A fresh, sharp and imaginative critique of South Africa's development trajectory since 1994 by one of the country's most incisive minds. A very important contribution to South Africa's post-apartheid development discourse. — **William Gumede**, Honorary Associate Professor, Graduate School of Public and Development Management, University of the Witwatersrand.

SOUTH AFRICAN
DEVELOPMENT
PERSPECTIVES
IN
QUESTION

The conflicting nature of people,
environment and
development

Leslie Dikeni

REAL AFRICAN PUBLISHERS

First published in 2012 by Real African Publishers
The Mills
66 Carr Street
Newtown 2001,
Johannesburg,
South Africa

© June 2012

© Leslie Dikeni

ISBN 978-1-920222-43-7

Editor:	Umakrishana Kollamparambil
Copy editor:	Angela McClelland
Index:	Jackie Kalley
Book design:	Mad Cow Studio
Cover design:	Adam Rumball

Financing: A special thanks to SAFIRI for their generous support of the project

Author photo: Reedwaan Vally

Printed and bound in South Africa

Set in Minion 12pt and Frutiger

Contents

Dedication

TO MY LATE PARENTS

Magdeline N Dikeni and George N Dikeni

Thank you....!

I am Sorry...!

Leslie Dikeni

Acknowledgements

This work was carried out over a period of seven years in the different provinces of South Africa; mainly the Northern Cape, KwaZulu-Natal and the Eastern Cape. The time spent in the field varied from one province to the other and was determined by the geographical scope of each area.

The research work in the first chapter was done in collaboration with the South African Revenue Service (SARS). I am very grateful to Mr Adrian Lackay (then spokesperson of the organisation), Mr Giorgio and Mr Aidan Keanly for having provided me with the opportunity.

The three case studies were carried out in collaboration with the Department of Social Development of South Africa. I am grateful to Jacques van Zuydam and Leon Swartz from the Chief Directorate: Population and Development for their assistance in organising and conceptualising the study. Thanks to Eunice Nchoe and other office administrators who assisted with all the required logistical issues.

I am deeply indebted to the many fieldworkers in the three provinces who, in different ways, confided in me, shared their experiences with me, introduced me to their cultural way of life and tolerated my demanding questions as an ethnographer. Through them I learnt a lot about their social world and my own.

In KwaZulu-Natal, the local people in Mtubatuba helped me understand the social dynamics of the area in different ways. Philip Mkhwanazi from the Khula village provided me with a list of other people to talk to. The staff members of the Mayor's office in the Mtubatuba Municipality were very helpful in providing me with a database of important people to interview in the field.

Mr Lafras Uys from the Beach Action Committee (BAC) was very helpful in providing me with information related to their problems with the State. Mr Prince Fakude, a senior community conservation officer at the Greater St Lucia Wetlands Park, helped by providing me with further information on the relationship between the Parks Board and the local people residing in and around the park.

Dr Kobus Herbst from the Africa Centre provided me with information regarding the impact of HIV/AIDS, malaria and other diseases on the local people residing in the area. Mr Rick van Wyk, an environmental consultant working with the Department of Environmental Affairs (now called the Department of Environment and Tourism) provided me with valuable information regarding the timber industry and the effects thereof on the forests.

The Manager of Cape Vidal camp provided me with other contacts within the Parks Board with whom to speak and shared his vast experience of working in the park.

I am indebted to various members of the Bethelsdorp Development Trust (BDT) in the Eastern Cape for their assistance. Mr Robert Gallagher, Executive Trustee, and the Chairperson, Mr Ronald Niegaardt, provided me the opportunity to analyse their organisation and helped by financing part of the study. Mr Rodney Boesak, the organiser, helped me identify key people within the organisation — and the community — for interviews.

Finally, Mr Elden Bonaparte and other members of the Trust helped a great deal in educating me about the various ways in which the Trust functions and, in particular, the different interfaces it has with government, business and other non-governmental organisations (NGOs).

During the initial stages of the study in the Northern Cape, I was assisted by Mr MC Lawrence, who served an internship with the Department of Social Development as part of his studies at the American University in Washington, DC. He was also mentored by Lead International, an international non-governmental organisation, the aim of which is to create networks amongst mid-career professionals involved with sustainable development issues.

Mr Themba Dlamini, research manager of the Department of Social Development in the Population Unit, joined the process during the final stages of the study. He helped in facilitating other meetings with relevant government departments within the province.

In the field, members of the Platfontein and Schmitsdrift communities helped me in various ways to understand the social, political and historical dynamics of the area.

The meeting that took place in Schmidtsdrift in 2004 among the various community members and organisations, such as the Communal Property Association (CPA) and the Council for Scientific and Industrial Research (CSIR) contributed to the research by providing a better understanding of the dynamics of land reform within the province and the two local communities residing within the area. Of importance here are the specific land claims by the affected communities against the State and commercial farmers.

Mr Mario Mahongwe from Platfontein helped us by organising a brief ethnographic visit of the area and identified key players who could assist us in assessing community perspectives and needs within the area. During the second phase of the study, his colleague, Mr Clifford Shaw, a commercial farmer and manager of the CPA, further provided us with information on wildlife farming, commercial farming, the management of ranges and conservation practices within the affected areas.

Mr Peter Mokomele, from the Land Claims Commission further exposed us to the specific dynamics of land reform within the area and helped us to draw some linkages between land reform processes and the process of environmental degradation within the area.

Mr Godfrey Mfetwa of the then Provincial Department of Minerals and Energy helped us to clarify the dynamics of mining and the impact thereof on the environment, the land reform process and the livelihoods of the local people.

Mr George Tina, Head of the Provincial Department of Local Government provided us with information on the process of service delivery within the area.

Mr Johan Lubbe from Plan Proactive, a regional town planning organisation, spent a lot of time informing us and exchanging ideas on the problems related to the environmental degradation process in the area, and how these impact on the process of development within the two affected areas.

Mr Andrew Morekwa, a member of the conservation community also provided us with valuable information on the different conservation practices within the area and how these affect the people living there.

Mr Darryl Koch, from the Provincial Department of Social Development, was responsible for data and information within the department and he helped us a great deal with local logistics and the required statistical data about the area.

Finally, Mery-Joy Schippers and Chriss Mpisi from the South African San Institute (SASI), a service provider to local communities within the area, helped a great deal with logistics and, more importantly, became at a later stage in the study, our sounding board for verifying data and our collected findings.

Writing this book gave me both a sense of fulfillment and dissatisfaction. Fulfillment because of the opportunity I had of living in the Netherlands and the numerous encounters with the many sociologists at the University of Wageningen, and in particular, the Department of Sociology of Development. To a great extent, my social and intellectual life was greatly influenced by these sociologists. It is through these people that I began to develop my own sense of intellectual indentity and was thus able to produce this book; the challenge of trying to think with your predecessors and/or think beyond them is not an easy one.

Hence, my sense of dissatisfaction is due to the feeling of not having met the challenge!

I am grateful to Professor Jan Douwe van der Ploeg, D Papadopulos, G Verschoor, P de Vries and Professor Norman, all of whom took a critical and reflexive stance in understanding the social world. I am especially indebted to Dr Alberto Arce for understanding my stubbornness and argumentative character and for helping me find my way. With him, I share the passion of understanding knowledge as a "social construct".

I am indebted to the Department of Political Science and the Department of Sociology at the University of Pretoria for allowing me the intellectual space, time and support for concluding this project.

Professor Husain Solomon helped by introducing me to the University and encouraged me to write. Professor Maxine Schoeman (though not a sociologist) welcomed me and gave all the necessary support to the project. Professor Janis Grobbelaar (a sociologist) hosted me and was always available to listen to my grumblings about how financial constraints negatively impact on my work.

Not to forget a friend and colleague from Italy, Professor Nicola Viegi, an economist from the University of Pretoria who was always available for a Sociology and Economics "boxing match" over a cup of coffee.

My sincere appreciation to Uma Kollambarambil for diligently editing my manuscript.

To my publishers, Angela McClelland and Reedwaan Vally, a big thank you.

In closing, the difficulty with projects of this nature is the scarcity of resources with which to complete the task. The financial constraints were a burden, especially in the absence of a regular salary. I would not have been able to complete this task without the generosity of so many of my colleagues in terms of material and moral support, and is this regard, I must thank the following people: Pingla Udith, Karuna Mohan, Seeraj

Mohamed, Lee Walters, Robert David Gallagher, Monde Juta and Maxwell Ramagoga. They all, in different ways, supported me materially and morally during the process of writing… and they did so without a trace of doubt or hesitation.

Finally, I am most grateful to Professor Andries Oliphant, for his unwavering support of the project. He truly has proven to me that as intellectuals we should not seek to "gain or lose face". The battlefield for ideas is one that we do not win through arrogance and ego. Rather, we do so through ideas, debate and engaging with each other. Please continue to engage in discourse with me, Ndlovu!

Thank you.

Leslie Mxolisi Dikeni

Preface

The period of the late 1970s and early '80s can best be described as a turbulent era in the history of South Africa. The banning of the black consciousness movement, the racial conflicts that divided the country, the mass revolts within the black townships and the State repression that engulfed the country, are all events that serve as attestations of how politically charged this period was.

Events outside South Africa's borders were no less dramatic. After a protracted struggle, Angola and Mozambique gained their independence from Portugal, and South Africans saw the advent of Afro-Marxist states on their borders. The bush war in Rhodesia finally ended with Robert Mugabe winning a landslide victory at the polls and the birth of Zimbabwe as a socialist State. For some South Africans these newly independent states were an apocalyptic sign of an impending communist victory in the region. For others, they were a sign of hope for political liberation and economic equity in South Africa (Leatt et al., 1986).

It was during this ideologically-charged environment that my social and political consciousness was shaped. Many South Africans of this generation will admit that this environment heightened the ideological conflict in South Africa and has had a great impact on their political and social lives.

During this period and for many years to follow, there were different contending ideological and theoretical perspectives within the country. These perspectives conflicted with each other and can best be described as "critical", "positive" and "neutral".

From a critical perspective, ideology is biased; it's an over-simplified, emotional expression of prejudice by a section of the public. More precisely it is a legitimisation of a particular group interest.

The positive perspective sees ideology as a socio-political charter, a vehicle for political propaganda designed to win converts to a particular political programme.

The neutral stance strives for a non-evaluative approach to ideology, claiming that all systems of thought are ideological by definition.[1]

In my view, based on my limited experiences, there were different contending dominant ideological schools of thought during this period. These are: Black-Consciousness, Liberalism, Afrikaner Nationalism, African Nationalism and Ethnically-Black Nationalism.

My intention here is not to deal with the specific and wider historical political perspectives of these different contending ideological schools of thought. Suffice to say that, all schools of thought, in their different and contrasting ideological positions, held different perspectives with regard to the South African political, historical economic debate at the time. Leatt et al. (1986) document these ideological perspectives in detail.

Briefly described, these schools of thought are: the liberal market school of thought, various radical or revisionist approaches, and the black anti-racist opinion, which may lean towards either the liberal or to the radical school while drawing on traditional African values.

Within the Black Nationalism group of social actors and/or camp (which I obviously was part of) there were differing ideological emphases towards resolving South African historical, socio-political problems. These differences were popularly known as differences between the charterists and the Africanists (often characterised in a dichotomous way by the media and other groups as charterists versus Africanists). The former group of social actors based its ideological perspective on the philosophical foundations of the Freedom Charter, which espoused a mixture of classical liberalism and modern African socialism, and also envisaged a non-racial democratic

---

1. For a further reading on these theoretical ideological perspectives, see Leatt, Kneifel and Nurnberger 1986).

South Africa.

The latter group of actors, in contrast to the former regarded the Freedom charter as a denial of Africanism, as espoused by many other post-African liberation movements that existed during this period. However, the objectives of the Africanists' policies was to envisage a future South Africa in which all are Africans [regardless of their colour].

Despite the different ideological political emphases held by the different political and social actors within the group of Black- Nationalism actors, there were commonalities held by these various social actors on the political and economic questions of South Africa. Roughly and briefly described, the politico-economic ideological viewpoints of these social actors espoused a socialist ideology perspective in all its different forms (i.e. populist and scientific) and essentially were proponents of a centralised politico-economic model for development. Such a perspective was in direct contrast from the politico-economic ideological perspective held by the liberal market school of thought, which was a proponent of a free market capitalist economy for development.

Of importance here, is the tracing of my own historical, political and ideological trajectory, which was largely influenced and shaped by these other ideological perspectives. It was indeed these theoretical ideological perspectives that to a large extent shaped my political ideological consciousness as an activist within the Mass Democratic Movement (MDM) and an under ground member of the then banned African National Congress (ANC).

I admit that during this period, my own theoretical approach to these debates was not based on a social scientific enquiry but rather on a strong and limited orthodox ideological foundation. In short, I was in support of a Neo-Marxist theoretical perspective (with a strong anti-capitalist approach!) that was in favour of non-racialism as a social formula for resolving South Africa's highly complex political and social problems.

My work travels as a fieldworker to South American countries, mainly Brazil, Peru and Bolivia, in the mid-80s further exposed me to the failures of capitalism as a political and economic system. On the other hand, they also exposed me to some of the struggling socialist projects there.

Linked to all of this were brief visits I had undertaken (for anti-apartheid work) to the erstwhile USSR, the former German Democratic Republic and some of the African countries that exposed me to state bureaucratic practices there. All of these experiences bothered me a lot and yet provided no theoretical answers to my questions.

Hence the emergence of the idea and curiosity about research methodologies that could help me clarify and find answers for my theoretical questions. My critical enquiry to research and the importance of research methodologies further left me with doubts and concerns about the empiricism of contemporary research methodologies (to which I was exposed at the time) used in South Africa and elsewhere.

It was only through my studies in the Netherlands, at the University of Wageningen, Department of Sociology of Rural Development, that I was able to partially find answers to my questions. Through debates with fellow students and lecturers, I was able to confirm my suspicions about the empiricism of some of the contemporary research methodologies used.

In Wageningen, I learnt to develop a theoretically grounded approach to social research that allows for the elucidation of actors' interpretation and strategies, and how these interlock through processes of negotiation and accommodation.

However, one of my concerns and interests has always been to find research methodologies that would enable me to make connections to seemingly unconnected things. Something I tried to achieve during my other research studies, but not entirely to my satisfaction.

One of the issues facing contemporary research methodologies is to find partial connections that can reconcile information contained in historical documents with the conceptualisations of various local actors as well as the descriptions, analyses and linkages of the observers of the text narrative. Hence, as we shall see later in this book, the ethnographic research methodological approaches adopted in conducting the various cases studies conducted in the different research sites.

My student days in Wageningen were not easy, since my theoretical perspective to development theory and practice was (as mentioned earlier) mainly based on limited orthodox Neo-Marxist politico economic perspective. And as I realised later, was highly influenced by the traditional structuralist/ institutional analysis that often was applied in South African development studies and elsewhere.

In this regard, Wageningen further exposed me to the theoretical and methodological foundations of an actor-oriented and social construction form of analysis. Such an approach is opposed to the traditional structuralist/institutional analysis and rather adopts a social constructionist approach to the challenges of development.

My pedagogical induction (indeed not without any struggle and resistance) to the theoretical methodological foundations of an actor oriented analysis in Wageningen further led me to other problems. And that is, after a brief visit to South Africa for research work, and through different encounters with some Neo Marxists colleagues I realised the enormous task of having to clarify and convince colleagues about using a different window of analysis in dealing with social problems of development (I failed!).

During this period, linked to the theoretical and conceptual problems I observed, there was also a very clear separation between theory and praxis amongst South African colleagues (e.g. we need to reconstruct the country and there is no time for these abstract theories). The key argument being that, social theories are not very useful for a process of policy formulation and development.

On my return to the Netherlands, the key theoretical debate (amongst some of my close colleagues) was on the relationship between theory and praxis and how these relate to policy implementation and social problems.

In questioning this relationship, we turned to the French Sociologist Pierre Bourdieu's work for a contribution on the debate. Bourdieu's work underlined that theory, empirical research and practical and policy dimensions are all interrelated and mutually dependent.

This contribution by Bourdieu to the debate further attracted me to his work and that of other French intellectual scholars. Despite a long-standing allegation that by surrounding himself with young dedicated followers, Bourdieu created a sectarian opinion machinery, I did not resist the temptation to pursue my intellectual project in France at Ecole des Haute Etudes Sciences Sociale (College de France).

This is where I further deepened my sociological theoretical and analytical perspective to development. As we shall see in the chapters to follow in this book, in College de France, Bourdieu's concept of a practice-oriented approach that is different from a structuralist approach and entails studying state intervention practices from an opinion of how the resources and meaning of intervention are appropriated by its agents, eventually leading to intervention coping, helped a great deal in my process of conceptualisation and theorisation of state intervention practices for development.

I was faced with the same dilemma on my return to South Africa in the mid-2000s that I had faced in the mid-90s of having to convince a wide variety of the so-called Marxist and Neo-Marxist colleagues (especially the orthodox Marxists who refused to think with Marx!) with whom I shared the same theoretical perspectives in a critical way. However, this time around, for obvious reasons, my theoretical approach to the engagement on the debate is pedagogical and didactical.

The idea of writing this book, therefore, arose from these debates, engagements and a concern for the need to re-think, re-theorise, re-conceptualise and question the South African development paradigm. Of importance here was to contribute to the ongoing developmental discourse on development in South Africa by elucidating and clarifying my theoretical conceptualisations of such a discourse. The courage of finally embarking on such a project would not have been possible had it not been for the encouragement of a colleague and friend, William Gumede. Recognising some of my frustrations at being misunderstood and my constant struggles of trying to verbally explain and clarify my theoretical thoughts and problems, he persuaded me to write!

Leslie Dikeni

Hatfield Pretoria, June, 2010

REFERENCE:
Leatt, J., Kneifel, T. and, Nurnberger, K. (1986) *Contending Ideologies in South Africa*. David Philip Publishers.

South African Development Perspectives In Question

CHAPTER 1

The Conflicting Nature of People, Environment and Development

INTRODUCTION

At present, there is an ongoing debate in many development conventions and conferences on the successes and failures of development projects in developing countries. What underpins these debates are (and which has been of key concern to me) the theories of development and intervention perspectives derived from the old theoretical paradigm on post-cold war development and social change.

The history of development intervention perspectives can be traced from the period of the 1950s with the conceptualisation of modernity, to dependency in the mid '60s, to political economy in the 1970s and to what others currently define as post-modernism since the '80s until today.

These theoretical viewpoints of the different stages of development, despite obvious differences in ideology and theoretical trappings, represent two structural models; modernisation theory and political economy. These have, until recently, occupied centre stage in the sociology of development and both evince paradigmatic and common analytical weaknesses.

The key actors involved in these debates are development experts, social researchers, state functionaries, international donor agents and environmental activists operating at different levels of society. The outcomes of these debates (by the actors involved) have a direct and/or indirect impact on the construction and implementation of development projects at different levels of society.

The South African development discourse has not escaped

this process of social scrutiny and forms part of the many project development case studies for debate.

On another level of public discourse, South Africa (especially its development discourse) has been seen by many at a local, provincial and national level of government as a successful development project story. Others, like the international donor agencies, journalists and those involved in international project management and evaluation, refer to it as a successful model of project management and development.

As will quickly emerge in the reading of this book, my purpose and interest in this study is to try and validate the different claims of success made by various government agencies (at different levels), international donor agencies, journalists and international development managers, in relation to the South African development trajectory.

Key to this process will be to understand how different local actors located in different parts of South Africa themselves respond to these claims. Of importance here is to understand the local actors' interpretations and perspectives of the South African development trajectory.

The study seeks to understand how these processes are translated by local actors and to comprehend the meaning and significance local actors give and/or attach to development projects in their area.[2]

In this book, the unmasking and/or problematisation of the so-called new development language and concepts currently used in the development discourse in South Africa are a central feature. The effect of this language in helping development projects to succeed or fail is an important issue that is examined in the book.

The manner in which different social actors organise, strategise, plan, act and thus, through this process shape development projects, with the aim of improving their lives, is

---

2. To do this, the concept of multiple realities will be employed as used by Luckmann and Schutz (1973). They describe how different actors accord different interpretations to the same situation or event, and thus construct differing social realities.

an important issue to be examined in this study.

Of equal importance in this book is the examination of the South African development process by the different external and internal institutions (e.g. state institutions, the private sector, development agents, etc.). The effects of these various institutional interests are examined in detail, in order for the reader to see, how these interests shape development projects with the South African development trajectory.

South Africa has a rich yet complex history that needs to be explored and examined. In the book a detailed examination and analysis of how that history has influenced and impacted on the current developmental processes in South Africa is given. In agreeing with those authors and/or sociologists who share the view that Sociology has contributed to policy-making and theoretical development (See for instance, Chambers, 1994, Roling 1988, Richards 1985), I give a sociological theoretical account of the differing South African developmental perspectives and their historical trajectories.

THEORETICAL APPROACH

Unlike the structural, institutional and political economy analysis of other general works in the field of development studies, this book focuses on the theoretical and methodological foundations of an actor-oriented and social-constructionist form of analysis.

The actor-oriented approach is an approach that allows for the elucidation of actors' interpretation and strategies, and how these interlock through processes of negotiation and accommodation. An actor-oriented approach places actors at the centre of the stage and rejects linear, deterministic and simple empiricist thinking and practices. An actor-oriented approach entails recognising the multiple realities and diverse social practices of various actors and requires working out methodologically how to get to grips with these different and often incompatible social worlds (Long, 1992, 5-6).

The actor-oriented approach can also be conceptualised as a social interface. A social interface is defined as a critical point of intersection or linkage between different social systems, fields or levels of social order where structural discontinuities, based upon differences of normative value and social interests, are most likely to be found (Long 1989, 1-2). In studies of the interface, the interface appears as a local of interaction. However, contrary to its original inception, the interface also seems to emerge as a boundary dividing two sub-systems, whose actors (e.g. state functionaries versus trust members and/or project implementers) have separate and conflictive cultural dispositions. However, one may argue that, a problem related to studies concerned with social interface is the supposition that the interaction at the interface is indeed crucial in ongoing processes of change at a local level.

This may lead researchers to neglect the other fields of activity or to underestimate the importance of actors who do not directly act at the level of the interface. During the process of research of this study, I accommodated some of these problems and tried to develop an approach that would take into account all the actors involved in the process of development.

The key actors involved in the process of project development within the South African developmental discourse are the State (in the form of local, provincial and national government), local people in different localities, national and international development agencies, and the private sector. All actors have a direct and/or indirect impact and interest in the development process of South Africa and/or its population.

The South African state, as the key actor, has the responsibility of having to interface with all these actors. These interfaces sometimes take the form of negotiations and strategising for projects and planning and implementing projects. Seen in this sense, the South African state has to navigate between the different actors with their different forms of power.

Hence, in this book a detailed account of the different interests that these individuals and groups have on the South African development discourse is given. Key to this process is to account for the different forms of contestation over resources for project development that are taking place amongst the actors involved in South Africa. Equally important is to examine the different internal and external conflicts that may be taking place amongst the different actors involved within the country, and comprehend how these shape and/or break the process of development currently taking place within South Africa.

All actors involved within the South African development discourse, have different historical trajectories (this also implies a knowledge of politics) that may have an impact on the development process and have shaped the outcomes of the development processes in South Africa. Therefore, key amongst the other concerns of this book is to examine and give an account of how those historical trajectories have shaped, re-shaped project development processes in the country and what can be observed from those processes.

In short, this book examines the different claims of successes attributed to different South African development trusts and agencies and endeavours to understand the interests of the different groups and individuals in the project development processes of these trusts and agencies, and the local people they represent.

This book gives a critical account based on local actors' interpretations of what constitutes a successful and/or an unsuccessful development project. Key to this process is the unmasking of different popular development concepts like sustainability, capacity building, project cycle, and scientific projects often used to characterise present-day development projects.

Equally, the way social actors interpret, translate and give meaning to these concepts is an important issue to be examined in this study. The important issue of how external and internal agencies (e.g. the State, international donor agencies) negatively and/or positively affect the development processes of the local people is an issue that is explored in this book.

Since the history of South Africa is characterised by different forms of political struggle, the different social actors involved in the South African development discourse hold different political historical trajectories. The book explores this through different ethnographic cases studies, with the view of understanding and showing how historical political processes influence and/or shape processes of development projects in different localities within South Africa.

The argument being that political historical process and the way history evolves does shape or influence outcomes of development projects at a local level and, thus, sustain them.

I am interested in developing an understanding of how local historical struggles in South Africa and perhaps elsewhere have shaped and, re-shaped the outcome of current development projects in different localities. How did the political actors involved in those struggles contribute to the shaping of the outcomes of current developmental processes in localities? What effect do the intervention practices of the State and external agencies have on these processes? Did the State and the external agencies take into account these historical processes?

Of importance in this book is the examination of the historical knowledge constructed by a variety of local actors' involvement in political "struggle" and how this form of knowledge has contributed in the shaping of development projects within different social contexts. Furthermore, how actors (involved in political struggles) perspectives can shape and/or break development programs and projects within localities are also examined.

An account of the way political struggles have influenced project development processes within different localities is given within the book. Key to this process is an account of the meaning different social actors located in different localities attach to project development within their areas. The ways in which different actors interpret and conceptualise the different development projects established by the State and other external parities within their areas is highlighted in this book. The important issue of what political and cultural meaning different actors attach to the different developmental projects currently taking shape within the different areas is given prominence in this study.

Of relevance to this study is a sociological account of how neutral descriptive development terms such as "scientific projects", "sustainability", "project cycles" and "capacity building" can enhance and/or slow down development processes. The important issue of how ideologies and political struggles impact on development processes is explored in the book.

An account of the central issue of how different social actors conceptualise and respond to the implementation of different development projects within different localities, and may thus engage in contestation of images and discourse on the meaning of how to implement development projects within localities is given.

The dominant theoretical paradigm of planned intervention in the 1960s and 1970s espoused a rather mechanical model of the relationship between policy, implementation and outcomes. The tendency in many studies was to conceptualise the process as essentially linear in nature, implying some kind of step-by-step progression from policy formulation to implementation to outcomes, after which one could make an ex post facto evaluation to establish how far the original objectives had been achieved (in other words, what are the strengths and weaknesses of a particular development project and what can be learnt from them?).

In this book, the impact of these historical paradigms on the South African development trajectory are explored and examined. The book explores "planned" and "state" intervention practices currently used in South Africa through different case studies, and illustrates their impact within its development discourse through an ethnographic field[3] research method. It is argued in this book that these theories are a key component of the concept of a Developmental State in South Africa.

Finally, the study seeks to develop further on the work conducted by other social scientists such as Law (1986), Latour (1986) and Callon (1986) in the sociology of science. The theory they put forward is not a given one of "how do we explain the success of science", rather how is science capable of transforming the social and natural worlds by enrolling a variety of actors (not only human in nature but also elements of nature itself and thought) within an actor network, translating their interests and finally producing passive agents who cannot do anything else but think of themselves, or define themselves in terms of the categories concepts and explanatory frameworks proposed by science.'

It is argued by this new approach to the study of science that the power of science lies in these social processes of translation and enrolment, and not in its being a kind of knowledge that is intrinsically superior to other forms of non-scientific knowledge. Science then is analysed as a cultural system whereby a particular kind of authority is enforced. What previously was the power of religion, has been replaced in modern times by those who have the key to the authoritative representation of progress, development, etc. In a nutshell, they set out to show that scientific knowledge is not a universal and "true" knowledge, rather the outcome of a particular conjuncture and knowledge.

Here, the effects of these institutional interests are examined in detail, in order for the reader to see how these interests shape

---

3. This is in line with Bourdieu's (1977) practice-oriented approach. Such an approach is different from structuralist approaches and entails studying state-intervention from the opinion on how the resources and meaning of intervention are appropriated by its targets, eventually leading to the emergence of intervention coping.

development projects within the South African Development trajectory.

METHODS AND TECHNIQUES OF FIELD RESEARCH

Due to the nature of the field research, a detailed account and description of the culture of social actors in the field, their different conceptualisation and interpretation of various developmental projects, and an understanding of how historical processes have influenced the process of development within the areas under study, was required. To this end, I employed the method of ethnographic research[4]. This process involved the interviewing of key informants and the analysis of existing data amongst the key informants within the field.

The fieldwork also occasionally assumed an applied nature, with the active involvement of all the actors engaged in the construction and implementation of development projects. The methodology used was different from Participatory Action Research (PAR) and other methodologies similar to it. This is so because it has been pointed out that the actual coincidence of research and actions often results in recipe research, or that it overlooks power-and knowledge issues that interfere in the implementation of activities. (Long, 1992 and, Arce, 1993).

Since the fieldwork assumed an applied nature, the roles of research and implementation process were strictly separated. The basis for the application of the research was to enhance and develop discussion between the different actors involved. The discussions were used to validate research findings and the processes that emerged from these dialogues were subjected to ongoing research.

---

4. The researcher did not adopt the actors' points of view, but rather attention was paid to the actors' own language of explanation during the fieldwork process. See De Vries (1992) for an interesting critique of ethnographic forms claiming "to give voice".

Access Biographies

According to Kohli (1981:64), the biographical — or autobiographical — method is not only the methodological model for the (hermeneutic) understanding of the individuals' lives, but also the privileged way to historical, or social reality. The three-fold goals of the biographical method are to get access to the social life as comprehensively as possible, within (i.e. its meaning and subjective aspects), and in its historical dimensions (ibid: 63).

The access biographies were specifically directed to the local actors in the field. My intensions were to try and get local actors to speak openly about their own local experiences during the different negotiations they have had with the various external and internal institutions operating within the different areas under study. In the field, I followed their stories in a detailed manner, and observed how they coped with the array of interventions taking place within their area, how historically they have constructed their organisations, and how ideology and politics have influenced the processes of project development within the areas under study.

By constructing a process to ensure that the local actors speak openly and in detail about their encounters with the powerfully resourced actors during the different forms of negotiation processes they have had with them, I was able to unearth certain of their secrets.

This is in line with Michel Foucault's findings based on the discourse with prisoners he interviewed: '[t]he discourse of struggle is not opposed to the unconscious, but to the secretive... A whole series of misunderstandings relates to things that are hidden, repressed and unsaid... It is perhaps more difficult to unearth a secret than the unconscious' (Foucault, 1977: 214).

REFERENCES

Arce, A. (1993). *Negotiating Agricultural Intervention: Entanglements of Bureaurocrats and Rural Producers in Western Mexico.* PUDOC, Agricultural University, Wageningen.

Bourdieu, P. (1977) *Outline of a Theory of Practice.* Cambridge: Cambridge University Press.

Callon, M. Law, J. RIP, A (eds.) (1986) *Mapping out the Dynamics of Science and Technology.* Sociology of Science in the Real World. London: Macmillan.

Chambers, R. (1994) *The Origins and Practice of Participatory Rural Appraisal.* World development, Vol 22, No7: 953-969.

Foucault, M. (1977) *Language, Counter Memory, Practice.* Oxford: Basil Blackwell.

Kohli, M (1981) Biography: Account, Text, Method in D. Bertaux (ed.) *Biography and Society: The Life History Approach in the Social Sciences.* Studies in International Sociology 23. Beverly Hills: Sage.

Long. N (ed.) *Encounters at the Interface. A Perspective on Social Discontinuities in Rural Development.* PUDOC, Agricultural University, Wageningen.

Long, N. and A. Long (eds.) (1992) *Battle Fields of Knowledge.* Routledge London/ New York.

Luckmann and Schutz, T. (1973) *The Structure of the Life World.* Evanston Illinois: North West University Press.

Potter, J. and M. Wetherell (1987) *Discourse and Social Psychology: Beyond Attitudes and Behaviour.* London: Sage.

Pretorius, D. (2005) *Framework for Sustainable Development and the Identification of Socio-Economic Opportunities for Bethelsdorp.* Unpublished Paper.

Richards, P. (1985) *Indigenous Agricultural Revolution.* Hutchinson and Westview Press, London Boulder and Colorado.

Rolling, N. (1988) *Extension Science and Information Systems in Agricultural*

Development. Cambridge University Press, Cambridge.

Schutz A. (1962) *The Problem of Social Reality.* The Hague: Nijhoff Publishers.

Vries, P de (1992) *A Research Journey: On Actors Concepts and the Text.* In: N. Long and A. Long (ed.) *Battle Fields of Knowledge.* Routledge London/ New York.

South African Development Perspectives In Question

CHAPTER 2

The Developmental State Theories: South African Perspective

INTRODUCTION

I n the previous Chapter, I indicated that there exists debate on the successes and failures of development projects within developing countries. Similarly, there is also an ongoing debate taking place in many development conventions, research seminars and conferences on the term and/or concept of a Developmental State, and what that means for developing countries. One may further argue that the failures of implementing many development projects in developing countries might have resulted in the re-emergence of this debate on the Developmental State.

The key actors involved in these debates are social scientists, state officials, development experts, various NGO activists, journalists, public commentators and various cabinet ministers.

As already stated in the previous section, these actors operate at different levels of society; e.g. local level (or micro), regional level (or meso) and national and/or international level (or macro level). The interaction between these different levels is decisive; especially relevant is the interaction at a local level and national level. At the latter level, international goals and mechanisms for what constitute a Developmental State are outlined.

Furthermore, the outcome of these debates, has a direct and/or indirect impact on the construction, re-construction and organisation of States at the national and local levels. Seen in this sense, the debate on the Developmental State remains to be an intellectual discourse in different parts of the world at large, and, in particular, within the developing world.[5] The South African state (especially its different departments) has not escaped this social scrutiny and forms part of the general debate on the nature of a Developmental State.

The objective of this chapter thus, is to examine these debates, to understand the different meanings and interpretations attached by different social actors to the concept or term of the Developmental State. The chapter seeks to understand how a variety of social actors translate this concept in their different environments and what meanings and significance these actors give and/or attach to the concept/and or term.

The chapter tries to answer the following questions: 1) What effect does such a term and/or concept have on the capacity of the South African state to organise and develop economically? 2) What are the [historical] and [methodological] bases of the existence of the concept of a Developmental State[6]? In so doing, the chapter tries to enhance the public understanding of the relationship between fiscal citizenship and the concept and/or term of the Developmental State.[7]

Key to this process is to provide a theoretical framework for an understanding of what may or may not be a Developmental State. An important issue to be dealt with in this chapter is to try and unmask and/or problematise the concept of the Developmental State in relation to the South African state with a view to create a better understanding of the concept and see whether such a concept has any relevance for the South African

5. When referring to the discourse, much more is meant than the language people use when talking about state development practices. Thinking with Foucault (1973), I see discourse as a form of (institutionalised) social practice embodying a particular conjunction between knowledge and power. Indeed, in the course of this text, when talking about discourse, I mean discursive practices. Thus, official discourse refers to the discursive practices bureaucrats employ in particular situations for dealing with clients who are advancing their own institutional projects. The discourse of public administration refers to a particular way of speaking about, or representing, practices of governability. Public discourse refers to the ways in which arguments are constructed in a public debate.

6. Here, quite often many researchers and scientists tend to take for granted the use of concepts; in that they would use a concept without trying to understand the origins and the research methods used (if any were used at all) for constructing such concepts. Equally, they pay less attention to the methodological framework and/or principle that exists to base an analysis on such a concept. The same problem is assumed here about the term (what others refer to as a concept) "Developmental State".

7. Though we cannot fully analyse and follow the discourse on language here, the data collected in the field suggests that there are different and contrasting views on the issue of language with regards to referring to a Developmental State as a concept or a term.

development discourse, using the South African Revenue Service (SARS) as an instructive case for this study.

In so doing, the researcher will undertake a critical review of existing data on the concept of the Developmental State in this chapter. This is achieved by an examination of the resolutions of the Limpopo conference with a view to assessing whether the outcomes of such a conference have introduced a new and/or nuanced understanding of the concept of a Developmental State.

UNDERSTANDING THE DEVELOPMENTAL STATE

A growing body of different opinions and contrasting views in the form of data suggest that the Developmental State as a term primarily concerns itself with the ways and means of how a State governs, intervenes in the lives of its citizens, and organises and mobilises resources for itself in order to transform and effect economic and social change in society for developmental purposes. Equally relevant here is how the State relates to organised civil society groups, including the market, and how these groups relate to the State.

Other viewpoints of the term consider how the State intervenes in the market, and what policy methods the State uses to intervene in the market to be of critical importance. Key to this process is how the State plans, and through the process of planning, implements developmental policies in localities and elsewhere, with the objective of affecting changes in society.

The term, according to others, also has a historical trajectory that comes from Europe and Asia. Below is a brief summary of some of these opinions.

As we engage with the debate on the Developmental State, it is important to understand that different models have been informed by, and evolved through, diverse stages in human history. The first Developmental State emerged in the 16th century in the northern parts of the Spanish Netherlands, which evolved into today's The Netherlands (Bagchi, 2000).

The modern Developmental State appeared in the post-World War II period, with the emergence of newly independent countries in Africa and Asia. The international community then embraced a state-led model of development to bring about industrialisation and entrepreneurship through intensive and deliberate effort and State intervention. The Economic Commission for Latin America and the Economic Commission for Africa, formed in 1948 and 1958 respectively under the mandate of the United Nations, became leading examples of such an approach (Fritz and Menocal, 2006).

Developmental States have had to adapt themselves to local conditions and changing circumstances in order to remain relevant. One feature of a successful Developmental State is its ability to switch gears between market-directed and state-directed growth, depending on the economic and socio-political circumstances, or to combine them in a synergistic manner (Bagchi, 2000). Historical data has shown that State intervention is critical when dealing with the flux and imperfections of the markets. Successful Asian industrialising nations were very interventionist in trade, foreign direct investment technology transfer, and domestic resource allocation (Lall, 2003). The success stories of economic growth and socio-economic upliftment in East Asia are explained by particular State interventions in the market which, were driven by a coherent national development vision and the systematic deployment of administrative and political resources to the task of national development.

The 1980s witnessed a paradigmatic shift in the evaluation of the State's role to promote economic growth in the developing world. Against the backdrop of inefficient State intervention in Africa, neo-liberal policies dominated the international economic discourse. Those who embrace this view argue that anything the State can do, the market does better; that anything the State does will be offset by actions of the private sector; and that, by trying to improve resource allocation, the government interventions make matters worse; for example, through rent seeking. Therefore, they believe that the market should address such developmental problems as industrial growth, international competitiveness and employment creation (Saad-Filho, 2004).

According to Levine (2008: 28): 'in a Developmental State, the government leads a long concerted drive for economic growth, ensuring the mobilisation of national resources towards the development goals. Although a Developmental State prioritises and promotes development, it is a conjunctural configuration whose route and approaches are contingent on national history and the choices made by citizens and leaders. Many countries are examples of the Developmental State, including Germany under the Marshal Plan, post-colonial Uganda and the "Asian Tigers" (South Korea, Taiwan and Hong Kong). Those with a longer view of history include the 16th century Netherlands, England and Germany between the 1848 revolution and the First World War.'

The Developmental State project in South Africa is based on the recognition that the inequalities in our society would not be addressed through the operation of the market. Inequality in South Africa has manifested itself in the appearance of a dual economy. Colonialism and apartheid gave rise to a 'peculiar form of capitalism, [which] turned the African majority into a landless, property-less disenfranchised, unskilled labouring class'. This state of affairs has been exacerbated by the fact that, since the 1980s, the economy has needed fewer and fewer unskilled workers; thus 'this reservoir of cheap labour now overflows with the unemployed, the indigent, the old and the very young' (Mbeki, cited in Levine, 2008).

And according to Edigheji (2005), the democratic Developmental State embodies the principle and (practices) of electoral democracy and ensures citizen participation 'in the development and governance processes'. It 'can also foster economic growth and development', and has clearly defined socio economic objectives that require State intervention (including reduction of poverty, social justice, reduction in income and asset gaps between rich and poor), and development of institutional and organisational structures that enable it to promote and achieve better economic performance (Edigheji, 2005: 6-7).

Thus, 'structural adjustment programs (SAPS), crafted by the International monetary Fund (IMF), became the order of the day. Although in many cases these helped to restore macro-economic stability, they also had a detrimental effect on the State capacity. Areas that particularly suffered included the provision and delivery of basic social services, the maintenance and modernisation of the civil service and the financing of the State. Neo-liberal thinking offered little practical guidance other than outsourcing tasks to NGOs or public private ventures. In many cases, the privatisation of key economic sectors, such as telecommunications, energy and mining, was carried out in a rush and without transparent bidding processes leading to the creation of ineffective private monopolies, rather than increased market competitiveness' (Fritz and Menochal, 2006).

The failure of neo-liberal policies was nowhere more evident than in Africa. South African Police Services (SAPS) dismantled State capacity in the name of fighting bad, corrupt and inflated governance. As a result, the role of the State in both the economic and social sphere of society was systemically diminished, leaving them little capacity to engage in developmental efforts (Mukhithi, 2008).

'The disastrous performance of neo-liberal policies in advancing the development agenda calls for a redefinition of the role of the State. Drawing from the success of the East Asian and some African countries, the concept of a Developmental State has evolved to offer an alternative to the global developmental discourse dominated by western neo-liberal thinking'

(Mukhithi, 2008).

Although the Developmental States in East Asia were characterised by authoritarianism, the concept of a democratic Developmental State has since evolved. A democratic Developmental State is one that not only embodies the principles of electoral democracy, but also ensures citizens' participation in the development and governance processes (Edigheji, 2005).

SOUTH AFRICA AND THE DEVELOPMENTAL STATE: A THEORETICAL MODEL

Reflecting on the history (and also based on the outcomes of the African National Congress national conference which took place in Polokwane in 2007) of the South African development and transformation since the Freedom Charter and the failure to effectively affect social and economic change, Turok (2008: 3) notes that:

... 'What seems to have added fuel to the fire of resentment about government's performance, is that in every major speech and document, the government continues to claim a continuity of policy from the Freedom Charter to the RDP, to GEAR and to the present government surpluses. Yet, as the conference documents conceded, inequality has increased, violating the principle of the Freedom Charter that "The People Shall Share in the Country's Wealth".

According to him, 'all these concerns explain the repeated demands for a Developmental State, not merely as a policy objective, but as a reality. The masses of the people want development to be extended to them and to experience it wherever they are. The commonly used expressions "people-centred" and "people-driven", found in so many ANC declarations, have to be tangible'.

The ANC statement of 8th January, 2007 seems to have taken this on board and calls for 'a coherent strategy for a progressive

Developmental State.

Summarising and reflecting on the outcomes and deliberations of a high level seminar[8] organised by New Agenda on the request of the Minister of the Department of Local Government (DPLG) Sydney Mafumadi; Turok, (2008, p, 20) had this to report about the term Developmental State:

... Debating the role of the State in socio-economic development, the seminar highlighted the importance of provincial and local government and the need for appropriate capacity for planning and implementation. Rural development remains a major hurdle for the creation of a Developmental State: rural people have no "voice", and a vision for rural areas is sorely needed. The discontinuity between first and second economy, which has its origins in the apartheid era, needs to be bridged and government programs need to be fast-tracked. The seminar concluded that, in the absence of a comprehensive development strategy, South Africa could not presently be characterised as a Developmental State, but it has taken several steps in this direction.

A South African state must be a strong State, able to intervene effectively. But it must also be democratic, and in this respect it would differ from the authoritarian East Asian Tigers. Our external environment is also different from that which enables the East Asian State to advance so successfully. It is more fluid and contested. Also, theirs was marked by a strict control of labour, which is not the case in South Africa. It was suggested that the State has to build cooperation with labour and capital and overcome the elements of distrust between them (ibid: 21).

A Developmental State in South Africa should give considerable attention to provincial and local government and to rural development. Presently the provinces do not have the necessary competencies to guide development, such as capacity

---

8. Amongst many others, the objective of this conference was to discuss the meaning of the term Developmental State with the aim of reaching some form of consensus on the term. The conference was attended by senior policy specialists from the cabinet, the presidency, state departments, parliament, parastatals, labor and academia.

for planning and information. Nor do they have the resources to create the necessary agencies. There is also a deficiency in collaboration between the different spheres of government. The public service is compartmentalised — there is no joined up government that could lead to common outcomes (ibid: 23).

In South Africa, the Developmental State is characterised by its democratic content and the role of the State in socio-economic transformation. It prioritises both social and economic development and draws on participatory and integrated planning processes to undertake pro–poor, redistributive and proactive interventions. The emerging South African Developmental State is non-racial, people-centred and participatory. The Accelerated and Shared Growth Initiatives of South Africa (ASGISA) and related initiatives have placed the South African government on a "business unusual" footing for the last 18 months of the third term of democratic governance (Levine, 2008).

And again, according to Levine, in a Developmental State, State intervention is instrumental in overcoming market failures or imperfections, and thus needs to have bureaucratic capacity to intervene strategically, especially on behalf of vulnerable individuals and groups.

State capacity is widely seen as a defining element of the Developmental State, but the phrase is used liberally and is often misunderstood. It encompasses a number of areas, including financial, technological, intergovernmental policies and systems, and human resources. In order for the state to stimulate economic growth, it requires the financial resources to implement its developmental programmes, the technological infrastructure to make efficient use of its resources, policy frameworks to inform its activities, as well as competent people to drive the process. Each one of these elements is fundamental to the evolution of a nation and none of them should be ignored (Levine, 2008).

The Developmental State needs a strong centre

complemented by a capable administration, able to work in unison towards common socio-economic and political objectives. Where resources are limited, central planning with devolved implementation is critical to getting the right mix between centralised and decentralised authority and policy execution (Levine, 2008).

The achievements of a Developmental State must ultimately be measured by their capacity to promote shared, sustainable employment-generating development and growth in an environment that respects and nurtures democracy and democratic institutions. In South Africa, the Developmental State must be measured against the legacy of apartheid, which entails immense material deprivation, racialised poverty, racial segregation, a hugely unequal race-based division of land, wealth and income, and legalised, institutionalised, violent and systematic racial discrimination in all walks of life (Levine, 2008).

An alliance between the State, civil society and business is a fundamental necessity, but the State should lead the developmental agenda. Its ability to advance national development without being captured by particular interest is critical (Mukhithi, 2008).

The Developmental State we are building should lead and manage economic relations. It must have the capacity to respond to changing conditions. Relations with private capital should be premised on common interest, vision and struggle. State policy is a key variable in successful development outcomes, and its effectiveness is determined by the degree of embedded autonomy the State enjoys. The establishment of institutionalised channels for continual negotiation and renegotiation is important (Mukhithi, 2008).

THE DEVELOPMENTAL STATE AND SOCIAL CHANGE

Our discussions above, based on the growing body of different opinions with contrasting views, suggest that the "Developmental State" as a term, primarily concerns itself with the ways and means of how a State governs and intervenes in the lives of its citizens, and how a State mobilises and organises resources for itself in order to transform and/or effect economic and social change in society for developmental purposes. And that, equally, the ways and means of how the State relates to organised civil society groups, including the market and how these groups relates to the State, is the major emphasis of what constitutes a Developmental State.[9]

Furthermore, critical to some of the defined opinions of the term, is how the state intervenes in the market. Central to this process ,is how the State plans, and thus, through this process of planning, implements development policies in localities and elsewhere with the objective of affecting social and economic change in society.

Key to some of my theoretical arguments in this chapter is that there is nothing new about the term "Developmental State"; that there is nothing that has not been said before about these definitions and characterisations of State-led social change and development processes. Whilst the origin of the term derives from Asia and Europe there are no theoretical and methodological bases for the existence of this term.

Furthermore, theoretically and conceptually thinking, the term cannot be seen and/or be used as a concept, neither can we attribute the meaning of a "theoretical model of development" to the term.

Rather, in my view, it represents a grouping together of a series of some loosely-related phenomena of "state" and "development" under the rubric of a Developmental State.

---

9. At this level of the debate, there is convergence of ideas amongst the authors.

Indeed, we are once again faced with some fashionable prescriptive phrase for development and social change.

As evident in the literature and the different bodies of opinion cited above, the term really is grappling with theories of development and intervention perspectives. These theories and perspectives on development intervention emanate from the old theoretical paradigm on development and social change of the post-Second World War.[10]

The genesis of the different theoretical viewpoints regarding the various stages of development processes is best explained in summary by a development sociologist, Norman Long. 'Despite obvious differences in ideology and theoretical trappings, two structural models have until recently occupied centre stage in the sociology of development viz., theories of modernisation and political economy. Both evince paradigmatic similarities and common analytical weaknesses.'(Long, 2001)

Modernisation theory visualises development in terms of a progressive movement towards technologically and institutionally more complex and integrated forms of modern society. This process is set in motion and maintained through increasing involvement in commodity markets and through a series of interventions involving the transfer of technology, knowledge resource and organisational forms; from the more developed world or [sector of a country] to the less developed parts. In this way, traditional society is propelled into the modern world, and gradually, though not without some institutional hiccups (i.e. what are often designated "social and cultural obstacles to change"), its economy and social patterns acquire the accoutrements of "modernity" (ibid: 10).

On the other hand, Marxist and neo-Marxist theories of political economy stress the exploitative nature of these

---

10. The concept of the paradigm, in its Sociological use, derives from Kuhn (1970) on the nature of scientific change. For him, scientists work within paradigms, which are general ways of seeing the world and which dictate what kind of scientific work should be done and what kinds of theories are acceptable. These paradigms provide what Kuhn calls "normal science", the kind of science routinely done day after day. Over time, however, normal science produces a series of anomalies, which cannot be resolved within the paradigm. Kuhn argues that at this point there is a sudden break, and the old paradigm is replaced by a new one, leading to a new period of normal science.

processes, attributing them to the inherent expansionist tendency of world capitalism and to its constant need to open new markets, increase the levels of surplus and accumulate capital. Here the image is that of capitalist interests, foreign and national, subordinating (and probably in the long-run undermining) non-capitalist modes and relations of production and, relating them into an uneven web of economic and political relations. Although the timing and degree of integration of countries into the world political economy has varied, the outcome is structurally similar: They are forced to join the brotherhood of nations on terms not developed by themselves but by their wealthier and developed "partners". Although this type of theory contains within it a variety of schools of thought, in essence the central message remains much the same, namely that patterns of development and under-development are best explained within a generic model of capitalist development within a world scale (ibid: 10-11).

These two macro perspectives represent opposite positions ideologically — the former espousing a so-called "liberal" standpoint and ultimately believing in the benefits of gradualism and the trickle-down effect, and the latter taking a radical stance and viewing development as an inherently unequal process involving the continued exploitation of peripheral societies and marginalised populations. Yet on another level, the two models are similar in that both see development and social change as emanating from external centres of power via interventions by the State or international bodies, and following some broadly determined developmental path, sign-posted by stages of development or the succession of different regimes of capitalism. These so called "external" forces encapsulate the lives of people, reducing their autonomy and, in the end, undermining local or endogenous forms of cooperation and solidarity, resulting in increased socio-economic differentiation and greater centralised control by powerful political groups, institutions and enterprises. In this respect it does not seem to matter much whether the hegemony of the State is based upon a capitalist or socialist ideology, since both entail tendencies towards incorporation and centralisation. Both models therefore are tainted by determinist, linear and externalist views of social change (ibid: 11).

Key to some of the theoretical underpinnings of this paper (and as already mentioned elsewhere) is that this process of grouping together a series of loosely-related phenomena of "development" and "state" under the rubric of a Developmental State, is in fact a recycling of old theory. This rubric of phenomena on the Developmental State in my view is a continuation of the old theoretical models of development so well characterised and defined by Long (2001).

In other words, this phenomena and/or definitions are propelling us to view development and social change in a deterministic and linear way and thus forcing us to adopt an externalist view of social change.

It is my belief that the concept of an actor-oriented approach is methodologically and theoretically best suited for exploring issues of State intervention and development change. This is so because such an approach serves as a counter-point to structural analysis and development models that are deterministic and linear and thus view social change from the point of view of the actors involved. At this point, it becomes important for us to re-capture and remind ourselves about the basic theoretical framework of such a concept as previously articulated by Long in Chapter 1 of the book.

'The actor-oriented approach is an approach that allows for the elucidation of actors' interpretation and strategies and how these interlock through processes of negotiations and accommodation. This approach entails recognising the multiple realities and diverse social practices of various actors and requires working out methodologically how to come to grips with these different and often incompatible social worlds.

The actor-oriented approach can also be conceptualised as

social interface. A social interface is defined as a critical point of intersection or linkage between different social systems, fields or levels of social order where structural discontinuities, based upon differences of normative value and social interests, are most likely to be found.'

It is through this foregoing theoretical and methodological framework that we examine the interrelations between the South African State, the South African Revenue Services (SARS) and its role within processes for social and economical change and development.

THE DEVELOPMENTAL STATE AND SOCIETY

Developing an enhanced and/or better understanding on the notion of a "fiscal citizenship" is a research question on its own. It demands to be studied ethnographically as a case study and not through a limited method of data analysis and the interpretation thereof. In other words, a practice-oriented approach is required here[11]. Especially since the concept concerns itself with state intervention. Suffice here to offer a brief theoretical and methodological approach of how we should understand such a term in relation to the state and its developmental process.

The phrase "fiscal citizenship" implies and/or is associated, amongst other things, with government finances, especially taxes. In practical terms this implies understanding how the State collects taxes from the citizenry in order to create resources for itself for purposes of economic development and social change. It also implies understanding how the State and/or the methods the State uses to meet these objectives. In other words, how does the State collect revenue from the citizens? What methods does the State use? And how do the citizens respond to

---

11. Such an approach, as conceptualised by Bourdieu (1977), is different from structuralist approaches and entails studying state intervention from an opinion of how the resources and meaning of intervention are appropriated by its targets, eventually leading to the emergence of intervention coping.

these practices by the State?

Fiscal citizenship, therefore, becomes an important theme for understanding how the State organises resources for itself for purposes of social and economic development. For understanding what methods the State uses to meet this objective and how the citizens respond to these actions by the State.

In the case of the South African Revenue Services (SARS), we shall assume in this paper that the primary concern here would be with how the State collects revenue from its citizens, the method the State uses for the purpose, and the response of the citizens (either through compliance or non-compliance) to this intervention practice.

The foregoing analysis of the notion of a Developmental State has clearly helped to clarify that there can be no model, theoretical formula, recipe book or methodological prescription for understanding State intervention practices and the actual processes of development. The same analytical approach here would apply to our understanding of the term fiscal citizenship. Hence, the notion of a fiscal citizenship in this paper shall not be treated as an independent variable from the other variables of how the State organises itself socially and economically for developmental purposes.

Rather the approach to be taken here should be that of an understanding that the notion of a fiscal citizenship is an emergent property: It emerges out of the actual processes of how the State organises itself for economic and developmental purposes. In other words, it is interwoven with these organisational processes.

My working hypothesis is that key to some of the South African Revenue Service's (SARS) objectives is to enhance its effectiveness for revenue collection. This implies a concern for how various actors within SARS, individuals or groups, organise themselves around the management of State resources (i.e. revenue collection).

The general approach to studying this problem by most researchers can be classified as two categories. The first studies the assumptions behind government attempts to increase revenue, raising capacity for revenue collection through policy, and the way these policies are often implemented by SARS, the results achieved and the obstacles encountered during the process. The second approach, on the other hand, examines the public perceptions of State revenue collection, its legitimacy and the levels of compliance by the public.[12]

This methodological approach to the understanding of State and civil society relations, in my view, is a gross simplification of State and civil society relations. And furthermore, it homogenises these relations and is pre-emptive about the problems that may arise from these relations. It re-enforces planned intervention by the State and other intervening bodies.

My contention is that, as opposed to this methodological approach to the problem, we need to consider how different actors with different interests and often in conflict, attempt (for example) to default tax, and thus through this process sustain, or appropriate State intervention practices.

At the same time, we need to examine how State agents engage in a variety of practices for handling institutional problems and how (in the case of the SARS) it deals with different groups of tax payers. In this sense, the issue of revenue collection then becomes an emergent property: it emerges out of the struggles between the different actors involved.

As stated above, the notion of fiscal citizenship concerns itself, amongst other things, with the collection of revenue from the citizens for the social and economic development of a State. This implies at a methodological level, that we want to interpret social, political and economic change as an outcome of struggles that take place between groups of different and often conflicting social interests. Hence the need for understanding the different strategies often used by these various groups often in conflict.

---

12. For an example of an approach to this problem, see Friedman (2003).

Thus, in the case of SARS, we want to understand, for example, how company officials and taxpayers organise their livelihoods.

The current methodological approach critiqued here, reinforces the notion of planned intervention by the State and other intervening parties. State intervention essentially refers to the ways and means of how the state and other powerful parties intervene in a planned way in the lives of citizens. This covers formally not only the organised State agency but also other intervening parties, such as commercial companies and enterprises that attempt to control and organise production and engage in the commercialisation of different products. My proposal stresses the importance of looking at this problem methodologically in terms of the interactions between different local groups and the intervening actors and entities.

The above approach to this problem compels us to examine the relations between State and civil society. This also implies that we need to examine how the State intervenes in the lives of its different citizens.

Civil Society, Market and State Relations

The literature reviewed earlier reveals to us that the more customary approach to and/or perspective of studying state and civil society relations has often been to dichotomise the two. In other words, the conflict between the two is often depicted as State against civil society and/or civil society against the State. My argument is that this is too simplistic and that instead, the relations between the two are far more complex than often depicted.[13]

Civil society and State relations need to be studied from the perspectives of the actors involved and that of the NGOs and

---

13. For an illustration, demonstration and/or an example in practical terms of the conflicting nature of civil society groups and individuals with the State, see Chapter 2, where a narrative account based on an Ethnographic Research study, conducted within the area of Bethelsdorp in the area of the Eastern Cape, is given. The outcomes of this study show clearly how civil society groups deal with state-intervention practices by penetrating, obstructing and subverting the state bureaucracy and by forcing state representatives to negotiate the authority of the State.

bureaucrats involved. This approach differs from the customary perspective on the theme of State and civil society relations.

My argument (see, Dikeni, 2007a) is that, in studying these relations we need to focus on the struggles surrounding particular types of State intervention. Instead of focusing on issues concerning the structural incapacity of the State to transform the livelihoods of populations, we need to focus on the social practices by which State intervention is sustained.

Key to this argument is that State intervention includes institutional models on how to deal with civil society tactics and strategies by which organs of civil society cope with State bureaucracy. These models, strategies and tactics are often shaped in concrete and often conflictive situations in which civil society organisations and State bureaucrats develop rhetorical organisational skills. Thus, instead of probing into the manifest or hidden rational of State intervention, we need to focus our attention on the discursive ways by which notions of State authority are fashioned between State and civil society organisations.

As already stated, our primary concern and attention should be placed on trying to understand how bureaucrats engage in a variety of practices for dealing with different organs of civil society. On the other hand, we need to examine the ways and means of how different organs of civil society deal with state intervention practices by penetrating, obstructing and subverting the State bureaucracy and by forcing State representatives to negotiate the authority of the State.

Furthermore, the tendency to simply assume that State and civil society organisations differ, in that they have unequal access to State power, is one we need to move away from. Instead we need to try and understand how capacities to act are produced, reduced and obliterated by both State bureaucrats and different civil society organisations that deploy certain strategies and models.

Our analytical and theoretical approach to the relations

between State and civil society must try to show the kaleidoscope of bureaucrats, practices of intervention and civil society groups' and individuals' strategies for coping with intervention by resisting State intervention practices.

State Intervention: Planned Intervention

The literature reviewed thus far indicates that, amongst other things, the term Developmental State concerns itself primarily, with state intervention in society. However, as alluded to earlier in this book, we not only need to examine the methods of intervention the state uses but also the strategies different social actors in the form of citizens are using in responding to State intervention.

A careful study of the literature indicates that most authors define State intervention essentially in a linear manner, prescriptive, diagnostic and formulaic manner. For example, terms like coordination, integration, planning, implementation, evaluation, etc., run across all the different definitions of a Developmental State by various authors. In a nutshell, the authors are proponents of what we can refer to as planned intervention.

The dominant theoretical paradigms of planned intervention in the 1960s and 1970s espoused rather a mechanical model of the relationship between policy, implementation and outcomes.[14] A tendency in many studies (which lingers on in certain policy discourses) was to conceptualise the process as essentially linear in nature, implying some kind of step-by-step progression from policy implementation to outcomes, after which one could make an ex post facto evaluation to establish how far the original objectives had been achieved. Yet, as any

---

14. By the 1980s there was a growing recognition of such deficiencies amongst policy analysts who sought new ways of conceptualising policy formulation and implementation (see Grindle, 1980 and Clay and Schaffer, 1984). It was argued, for example, that implementation should be viewed as a transactional process involving negotiation over goals and means between parties with conflicting or diverging interests, and not simply as an execution of a particular policy (Warwick, cited in Long 2001).

experienced planner or development worker will readily appreciate, this separation of policy implementation and outcomes is a gross over-simplification of a much more complicated set of processes that involves the reinterpretation or transformation of policy during the implementation process itself, such that, there is in fact no straight line from policy to outcomes. Also, outcomes may result from factors not directly linked to the implementation of a particular development programme. Moreover, issues of policy implementation should not be restricted to the case of top-down planned interventions by governments, development agencies and private institutions, since local groups actively formulate and pursue their own development projects that often clash with the interests of central authority (Long 1984: 177-9).

A careful analysis of all the theories outlined earlier on the term Developmental State by different authors, will indicate that these theories are trapped into the theoretical models of planned intervention that are clearly outlined by Long.

A central problem for analysis, therefore, is to understand the process by which intervention enters the life worlds of the individuals and groups affected, and thus comes to form part of the resources and constraints of the social strategies they develop. In this way, the so-called external factors become internalised and come to mean different things to different interest groups or to different individual actors involved, be they implementers, clients or bystanders.

These considerations lead to the conclusion that the concept of intervention needs deconstructing so that we recognise it for what it fundamentally is, viz., an ongoing, socially constructed and negotiated process, not simply the execution of an already specified plan of action with expected outcomes. The usual assumption is that decision makers, before they act, identify goals and specify alternative ways of getting there, assess the alternatives against a standard such as costs and benefits, and then select the best alternative (Long, 2001). This is often not the case, hence it is not enough then to modify or seek refinements of orthodox views on planned intervention, as is the case with theories of a Developmental State. Instead, one must break with conventional models, images and reasoning.

As was pointed out in Dikeni (2007b), we are now at a critical and exciting point in the South African transitional process, when old orthodoxies have largely given way to, or at least allowed room for, new modes of conceptualisation of the dynamics of social change and development. Sociologically, South African transitional process is pregnant with potentials for new forms of theorising and conceptualisations. The challenge for all of us is to think dynamically and not be trapped in theoretical orthodoxies. This belief is in line with Kuhn's view (1970) that social theorising and conceptualisation are not composed of one form of a singular paradigm but based on a multiplicity of paradigms.

DISCUSSION: CONCLUDING REMARKS

One of the issues facing contemporary research methodologies is to find partial connections, which can reconcile information contained in historical documents with the experiences and conceptualisations of a variety of local actors, descriptions, analyses and linkages of the observers at the level of the text narrative.

Hence, my concern has always been to find research methodologies that will be able to connect seemingly unconnected things (Dikeni, 1996). The key problem with this research study has been that the research method used has been one of collecting data, reading and re-reading it and, through that process interpretation of data, thus separating theory and praxis.

In this chapter I reconcile information contained in historical documents about the notion of a Developmental State in other parts of the world with that of different social scientists, and researchers of South Africa. I give an account of their descriptions and definitions of what the notion of a Developmental State means. Using the South African revenue Service (SARS) as an instructive case, the different meanings and interpretations attached by the various actors to the notion of a Developmental State are provided. The meanings and significance these various actors give and/or attach to the term is also illustrated in this chapter.

The important issue of understanding what effect such a term has on the South African state in its attempts to organise and develop itself is also examined in this chapter. Key to this process is to provide the readers with an understanding of the historical and methodological basis of the existence of the notion of a Developmental State.

This chapter developed a theoretical framework for an understanding of what might and/or might not be a Developmental State is given. An attempt has been made to try and unmask and/or problematise the notion of a Developmental State, in relation to the South African state, with the view to assess whether the South African Revenue Service (SARS) can better utilise the concept.

Key to some of my theoretical arguments in the chapter (and as the findings confirm) is the fact that there is nothing new about the term Developmental State and that there is nothing that has not been said before about these definitions and characterisations of state, and social change and development processes. The best meaning we can attach to the term is that of a fashionable prescriptive term for development and social change.

As evident in the literature and the different bodies of opinion cited in the chapter, the term really, is grappling with theories of development and development perspectives.

Hence, my argument that this process of grouping together the loosely related phenomena of "development" and "state" under the rubric of a Developmental State is in fact a recycling of old theory. Thus, I argue that these theoretical models on the Developmental State are trapped within two paradigmatic structural models for development evident within the periods of the 50s, the 60s and the mid-80s.

This points to the need for the concept of an actor-oriented approach in theoretically and methodologically examining problems of State intervention and development change. This is so because such an approach serves as a counter-point to structural analysis using development models that are deterministic and linear, and thus view social change from the point of view of the actors involved.

Similarly, developing an enhanced and/or better notion of a fiscal citizenship is a research question on its own. It requires to be studied ethnographically in the form of a case study and not through a limited data analysis and interpretation thereof. My emphasis here, is that such a process of research should examine this problem and/or issue within the broad context of understanding the State and its developmental processes for social and economic purposes. It requires a practice-oriented approach in the form of an ethnographic study.

The recommendation emerging from the foregoing theoretical and methodological framework, is that we should examine the interrelations between the South African state, the South African Revenue Service (SARS) and its role within the process for social, economic and developmental change.

This necessitates the need for us to deconstruct the concept of intervention (a key concern of the notion of a Developmental State) by the State and other parties and recognise it for what it fundamentally is, namely an ongoing socially constructed and negotiated process, not simply the execution of an already specified form of action with expected outcomes. This is true no matter whether it is within the market, and/or regarding the State intervention in local struggles between different and often competing and conflicting social groups.

REFERENCES

Alfredo S. (2004) From *Washington to Post-Washington Consensus: Neo-Liberal Agendas for Economic Development*, in Alfredo, S and D Johnston (eds.) *Neoliberalism: A Critical Reader*. London Pluto Press.

Bagchi, A. (2000) *The Past and Future of a Developmental State*. Journal of World Systems Research, VI, 2, Summer/Fall.

Bourdieu, P. (1977) *Outline of a Theory of Practice*. Cambridge University Press.

Clay, E.J. and Schaffer B.B. (eds) (1984) *Room for Manoeuvre: An Exploration of Public Policy in Agriculture and Rural Development*. London: Heinemann Educational.

Dikeni L. (1996) *Habitat and Struggle: The Case of the Kruger National Park in South Africa*. Wageningen Agricultural University, The Netherlands MSc Thesis.

Dikeni, L. (2007a) *Regaining the Old Paradigm: The Debate over Civil Society and State*. Divuho: Journal for Intellectual Engagement, 1st Edition.

Dikeni, L. (2007b) *BDT Perspectives: Equality, Service Delivery and Capacity Building, Challenges for South Africa*. Concept Paper, Pretoria, Development Bank of Southern Africa.

Edigheji, O. (2005) *A Democratic Developmental State in Africa?* A Concept Paper. Johannesburg, Centre for Policy Studies.

Friedman, S. (2003) *Culture, Tax Collection and Governance in South Africa*. Policy: Issues And Actors, Vol. 16, No 3. Centre for Policy Studies, Johannesburg.

Fritz, V and A Rocha Menochal. (2006) *(Re)building Developmental States: From Theory to Practice*. Working Paper 274 Overseas Development Institute, London.

Foucault, M. (1973) *The Order of Things*. New York: Vintage.

Grindle, M. (ed.) (1980) *Politics and Policy Implementation in the Third World*. Princeton. NJ: Princeton University press.

Kuhn, T.S. (1970) *The Structure of Scientific revolutions*, 2nd ed. Chicago

University Press.

Lall, S. (2003) *Reinventing Industrial Strategy: The Role of Government Policy in Building Industrial Competitiveness.* Working papers, Queen Elizabeth House, Oxford University.

Levine, R. (2008) *Public Service Capacity and Organisation in the South African Developmental State.* New Agenda, Issue 29, First Quarter.

Long, N. (1984) *Creating Space for Change: A perspective on the Sociology of Development.* Inaugural Lecture, Wageningen: Agricultural University. Revised version in Sociologia Ruralis, XXIV, 3-4: 168-84 .

Long. N (ed.) 1989 *Encounters at the Interface. A Perspective on Social Discontinuities in Rural Development.* PUDOC, Agricultural University, Wageningen.

Long, N. and A. Long (eds.) (1992) *Battle Fields of Knowledge.* Routledge London/ New York.

Long, N. (2001) *Development Sociology Actor Perspectives.* Routledge London.

Mukhithi, L. (2008) *A Democratic Developmental State: Driving the National Developmental Agenda.* New Agenda, Issue 29, First quarter.

Turok, B. (ed.) (2008) *The Message from Polokwane.* New Agenda, Issue 29, First Quarter.

South African Development Perspectives In Question

CHAPTER 3

.

The Case of the Bethelsdorp
Development Trust: In Question

Livelihood Strategies, State Intervention Practices, Local Knowledge and Development Projects

INTRODUCTION

This chapter will probably disconcert consumers of standardised theoretical and conceptual frameworks for local development process and disappoint those expert researchers who are in search of answers through a simplified formulaic research methodology. My intention here is not to produce a recipe book; neither do I intend to produce methodological or theoretical prescriptive concepts for complex social development problems through this chapter.

As discussed in the earlier chapters, most development practitioners, state agents, development agencies and sometimes NGO officials often measure the successes and failures of development projects by assessing their strengths and weaknesses using variables like equality, service delivery and capacity building. In this chapter I argue that this approach to development intervention practises turn out to be simplistic and linear in nature.

My point of departure is that equality, capacity building and service delivery have to be examined from the perspective of development projects and by taking into consideration of how this process affects the three variables outlined.[15]

Hence, in this chapter, we will examine how project development within the Bethelsdorp context affects the lives of

---

15. Projects in this paper are conceptualised as arenas of struggle for scarce resources (Bierschenk, 1988, Crehan and Van Oppen, 1988 and Van Dusseldorp, 1993).

local people within the area and thus through this process shapes and re-shapes their life worlds[16]. Of importance here, is to examine how local people socially benefit from project development within the area and what meaning they attach to the process of project development.

In other words, the question asked is how the Bethelsdorp Development Trust (BDT) affects service delivery within the area. Equally important is to examine and/or assess what capacity exists at a local level for service delivery and project development.

In this chapter, the central issue addressed is how different social actors conceptualise and respond to the implementation of development projects and engage in contestation of images and discourse on how to implement development projects within the Bethelsdorp area. Key to this process is to explore how different social actors conceptualise state intervention within the area.

The common and conventional approach to project development and the process of the implementation of projects, is often to set goals, objectives and establish programmes for implementation and thereafter assess strengths and weaknesses (and/or what lessons to be learned from them?) of the project concerned. This approach to project development, as argued in this chapter, is a mechanical model of the relationship between project, project implementation and outcomes.

The most dominant and conventional way with which knowledge is often associated, is to equate knowledge (both scientific and unscientific every dayforms of knowledge) with some professional, specialised or esoteric set of data or ideas. Equally, to some the goal of knowledge is to provide a literal account of what the world is like. In this chapter, I will try to assess the different dynamics of knowledge that are taking place within the area of Bethelsdorp, with the view of showing and

---

16. A life world is a lived-in and largely taken for granted world (Schutz and Luckmann, cited in Long and Long, 1992).

providing an ontological different approach to knowledge.

To address these important questions we will draw our analysis from different Ethnographic case studies already conducted on the Bethelsdorp Development Trust (BDT) and through this processe outline the challenges for South Africa.

THE GENESIS OF THE BETHELSDORP DEVELOPMENT TRUST (BDT)

The Bethelsdorp Development Trust was established in 1994 after the first democratic elections in South Africa and after the first democratic local government elections in the Eastern Cape (Port Elizabeth). The Development Trust is a joint initiative of the Northen Areas Development Trust (NADT), now known as the Bethelsdorp Development Trust (BDT). The Bethelsdorp Development Trust forms part of Port Elizabeth (PE) and is situated in the Eastern Cape of South Africa and is part of the Nelson Mandela Metropolitan Municipality (NMMM).

The key objectives of the Trust, since its inception, have been to (amongst other things) restore the historical ownership of the indigenous peoples' claims to five hundred and sixty hectares (560 ha) of land, previously dispossessed from its original inhabitants (who are mainly, Coloured, Khoi and African people) and the redevelopment of this natural resource and asset into a nature reserve and heritage site.

The Bethelsdorp Community prides itself as historically being part of the Eastern Cape Province of South Africa. Its historical trajectory can be traced from the period of the 1800s when in 1802, the colonial government of the Cape was convinced by British missionaries in London, namely a certain Mssrs Van Der Kemp and Read, to establish a settlement for indigenous people to cater for their educational, social and religious needs.

Preliminary research findings suggest that during this period their lives were under constant threat by the encroaching Dutch settlers from Gamtoos[17] who, during this time, systematically dispossessed people from their land, reducing them to become drawers of water and hewers of wood. Seen in this sense, the local people of Bethelsdorp have a complex and yet interesting historical trajectory that needs to be explored.

However, today the people of Bethelsdorp have organised themselves in different ways and have established a Development Trust, whose target beneficiaries are mainly all its citizens and/or inhabitants. The Trust places emphasis on development for specific individuals and groups. These individuals and groups reside in areas like Chatty, Bethelsdorp, Zwide and Missionvale and are an estimated group of 350 000 people living within a seven kilometre radius from the project nucleus.

According to the trustees of the Bethelsdorp Development Trust (BDT), its current development strategy identified nine clusters aimed at creating sustainable development opportunities within the Bethelsdorp community. These projects are located within five broad sector plans. These are: (1) Economic; (2) Environmental; (3) Social; (4) Heritage, Sports and Recreation (5) Housing, Land and Infrastructure.

Trust Board members claim that since 1994, the council has spent in excess of R7million in infrastructure upgradation, which resulted in numerous part-time jobs. Furthermore, all of this funding went directly into the ground as the community contributed all their time and expertise as volunteers.

Finally, these community members are currently formally organised into the Bethelsdorp Development Trust (BDT), which is a non-profitable charitable trust and the legal community custodian and the "driver" of the Bethelsdorp Development Project (BDP).

At another level of public discourse, the Bethelsdorp

---

17. The Gamtoos River is the natural boundary to Jefferys Bay, situated on the west of Port Elizabeth (PE). It is an important agricultural zone and is the beginning of the Langkloof agricultural plains. It is popularly known as the birthplace and burial site of Sarah Baartman. This suggests that there are linkages between Bethelsdorp and Gamtoos.

Development Trust (BDT) has been seen by many at the local, provincial and national level as a successful development project story. Others, like the International donor agencies, journalists and those involved in international project management and evaluation, refer to it as a successful model for project management and development.

THEORETICAL DEVELOPMENTAL PROBLEMS WITHIN THE BETHELSDORP LOCALITY

My argument is that the actor-oriented approach is methodologically and theoretically the best method for exploring these developmental claims by external actors involved in the development process of Bethelsdorp. This approach can also be conceptualised as a social interface between the state officials versus Trust members and/or project implementers.

It is through this methodological, conceptual and analytical framework that we seek to validate the different claims of success made by different government agencies at different levels, including international donor agencies, journalists and international development managers in relation to the Bethelsdorp Development Trust (BDT). The current developmental processes in relation to the Bethelsdorp Development Trust (BDT) can be analysed based on the old paradigms on development intervention referred to in the previous chapter.

Key to some of the theoretical underpinnings of this chapter is that the current social development process taking place within the Bethelsdorp area is affected by the theoretical models of development discussed in Chapter 2. In other words, they are trapped into these theoretical models for development, which are deterministic, linear and adopt an externalist view of social change.

In the following sections of the chapter we will explore these views connecting theory and praxis by analysing information drawn from different research studies already conducted in Bethelsdorp.

SITUATING THE DEBATE: THE BETHELSDORP CASE

The Bethelsdorp population (and especially its development trust) has not escaped the process of social scrutiny, and forms part of many development project case studies for debate. Furthermore, the trust is currently deeply affected by different external intervening agents like the State in its local development discourse.

The key actors currently involved in the process of project development in the Bethelsdorp area are: the State (in the form of local, provincial and national government), local people, national and international development agencies (e.g. DBSA,) the private sector (e.g. General Motors & Standard Bank) and the Bethelsdorp Development Trust (BDT). All actors have a direct and/or indirect impact and interest in the development process of the Bethelsdorp community and/or population.

As the key actor, the Bethelsdorp Development Trust (BDT) has the responsibility of having to interface with all these actors. These interfaces sometimes take the form of negotiations for projects, strategising for projects, planning projects and implementing projects. Seen in this sense, the Bethelsdorp Development Trust has to navigate amongst different actors with different forms of power.

These interfaces and processes of navigation often lead to a contestation of resources for project development by the different actors involved in the process of development within the Bethelsdorp area. Of relevance here, is the impact of the internal and external conflicts (caused by the different actors involved) that are taking place within the area over project development, and how these shape and/or break the process of development currently taking place within the Bethelsdorp area.

As already indicated elsewhere in this chapter, in the following sections we will illustrate these dynamics through various case studies already conducted within the area and through preliminary Ethnographic research studies conducted within the area.[18]

BRIEF ETHNOGRAPHIC READING: LOCAL NARRATIVE[19]

Intervention Practices: Planned Intervention

My first face-to-face encounter with the Bethelsdorp Development Trust (BDT) took place in a research seminar in Mafikeng in the North West province of South Africa in 2007. The research seminar was organised by the Department of Social Development of South Africa through its population unit.

At the seminar, different local, national and international developmental organisations were requested to present papers on the successes and failures of their development projects. The Bethelsdorp Development Trust (BDT) was one such development organisation asked by the Population Unit of the Department of Social Development to deliver a paper on its successes and failures. The paper was delivered by one of the Trust's executive members, who refers to himself as an activist.

After the presentation, during the question and answer time, I posed the following questions to the activist:

'Surely amongst all the different claims of success there must be some failures? Explain to us what the failures are with regards to the project? How do politics affect you in your development

---

18. In the field, during the process of doing preliminary research, the researcher did not in any way adopt the different actors' point of view, but rather attention was paid to the different actors' own language of explanation. For an interesting critique of ethnographic forms that claim to "give voice", see De Vries, 1992.
19. For an interesting use of narratives in project evaluation and project analysis, see van der Does and Arce, 1994.

work? What relations do you have with local state institutions?'

These questions were further explored outside the meeting in informal settings. The end result was an invitation by the activist to visit Bethelsdorp, as there was a need to document the history of the Trust and to do an in-depth study of the area.

During the course of the fieldtrip in Bethelsdorp, in meetings between local government officials and the activist; I posed the important question regarding how local government organisations relate to the Bethelsdorp Development Trust (BDT).

During the discussion that followed my informant showed a sense of frustration and anger about my apparent ignorance of the local dynamics of the area. He immediately responded by saying that perhaps he needed to use concrete examples to show me what problems they have with Local Government and Metro officials when dealing with community issues.

My host went on to say: 'Our problem is that our state does not understand how we operate. And we sometimes do not know how to deal with them when they interfere in our local development processes. They (the State) like to plan for us and claim to be doing things for us, this, without consulting or understanding what we want. When it comes to the Metro, we always have to deal with the political dynamics of the state.

'You see Leslie, previously we used to work with a guy called Mike Kwanaite, who was from the ANC (African National Congress) and was heading the Local Economic Development section of the Metro, an important position within the Metro. This guy understood our activist experiences, he understood where we came from, and could also understand how we operate and thus, could work with us.

'OK! Now recently, we saw a sudden change in the administrative personnel of the Metro. Mike was removed from his position of heading the Local Economic Development (Portfolio Councillor) and was placed in a less significant position. They replaced Mike with a woman by the name of Van

Jaarsveldt who crossed the floor (crosstitute) from the National Party to the ANC. This woman had no activist experience, had no historical background on what we are about, she did not understand how to work with local communities and thus in my view was useless…! Government is actually paying and employing people to retard and destroy development and service delivery agents in our democratic state…

'You see, we have a service level agreement in respect of funding for local economic development projects in the Northern areas with the metro, of which the Development Bank of Southern Africa (DBSA) is also a part.[20] In short, the funding agreement is for a period of three years and is meant to support some of our projects. These are the Hand Weavers Project, Aristotle Guesthouse, the Small Business Incubator, and more. All projects are currently progressing at a fast pace, they have the support of the local community and they have the support of the African National Congress [The ruling party] as well as other political parties in the area.

'We needed more financial support from the Metro, in order for us to sustain our development work on the 'ground. The Metro was not prepared to fund the process and thus, we could not move forward. The Chairperson and I tried in vain to secure funding from the Metro to sustain our projects.

'It was only recently, that we found out that Mrs Van Jaarsveldt was the one who stopped the funding, despite the approval of the ANC caucus to fund BDT-LED projects over 2007/08 financial year. This woman further went to the DBSA, insisting that BDT must not be funded, because we are a "family organisation"' …

'Now, you tell me why is this happening? How can the state do this to us? Why intervene negatively and not positively? All the big claims about developing local communities and yet you

---

20. The metro committed itself to fund the Bethelsdorp Development Trust (BDT) an amount of R680 000 for the period of 2006/2007; the financial year ended on the 30th June, 2007.

want to determine the pace of development and thus through this process destroy the organisation and deprive communities of resources…[21]

'It was only after she did this to us that we decided to respond to the situation by writing letters to the Mayor, by lobbying different political parties in the area and finally going out to the community and reporting these incidents. The community responded positively and immediately decided that we needed to set up a coordinating structure with other NGOs working in the Metro and surrounding areas for us to deal effectively with these issues.

'The strategy worked; today as we are talking there are negotiation meetings between us and different local state organisations to deal with the issue. The issue has even received the full attention of the Mayor…' (Fieldwork Notes: 2007)

BRIEF ANALYSIS

Intervention Practices: State Intervention Practices

The foregoing account shows us the nature of the relationship between the state (e.g. Metro) and civil society (e.g. BDT) within the Bethelsdorp area. Of importance here is the way by which the state intervenes in processes of development within the local area. In Bethelsdorp, what we are currently witnessing is the process by which the state intervenes in project development in a planned way. In response to this, the Bethelsdorp Development Trust (BDT) reacted, in various ways, to this form of intervention by the state.

This social drama between the Bethelsdorp Development Trust and the officials of the Metro indicates to us the way state bureaucrats are engaged in a variety of practices for handling institutional problems and for dealing with various groups of

---

21. These views carried support from various members of the Bethelsdorp Development Trust and local people in the area. Letters of correspondence between members of the BDT and the mayor's office also indicate these problems.

beneficiaries within the Eastern Cape province of South Africa.

They also show us the way the local people respond to state intervention practices by strategising, planning, sometimes obstructing and subverting state bureaucracy and thus, through that process forcing state representatives to negotiate the authority of the state. In other words, this shows us the kaleidoscope of bureaucrats, practices of intervention and local actors' strategies for coping with intervention by accom-modating or resisting it.

Hence, the need for us to deconstruct the concept of intervention so that we recognise it for what it fundamentally is: an ongoing, socially constructed and negotiated process; not simply the execution of an already specified plan of action with expected outcomes as often perceived.

Furthermore, what the story reveals and proves to us, is the way in praxis state and civil society relations within localities need to be studied. As already observed in the previous chapter, the more customary perspective of studying state and civil society relations has often been to dichotomise the two. In other words, the conflict between the two is often depicted as state against civil society and/or civil society against the state. My argument is that this is too simplistic and that instead, the relations between the two are far more complex than often depicted.

Civil society and state relations need to be studied from the perspectives of the actors involved — NGOs and bureaucrats involved. This approach differs from the customary perspective on the theme of state and civil society relations.

My argument is that in studying these relations we need to focus on the struggles surrounding particular types of state intervention. Instead of focusing on issues concerning the structural incapacity of the state to transform the livelihoods of populations, we need to focus on the social practices by which state intervention is sustained, resisted and appropriated.

Key to this argument is that state intervention includes

institutional models on how to deal with civil society tactics and strategies by which organs of civil society cope with state bureaucracy. These models, strategies and tactics are often shaped in concrete and often conflictive situations in which civil society organisations and state bureaucrats develop rhetorical organisational skills as this social drama shows.

Thus, instead of probing into the manifest or hidden rationale of state intervention, we need to focus our attention on the discursive practices by which notions of state authority are fashioned between state and civil society organisations, as evident within the social drama.

As already argued elsewhere in the paper, our primary attention should be placed on trying to understand how bureaucrats engage in a variety of practices for dealing with different organs of civil society. On the other hand, we need to examine the ways and means of how different organisations of civil society deal with state intervention practices by penetrating, obstructing and subverting the state bureaucracy and by forcing state representatives to negotiate the authority of the state.

Furthermore, the tendency to simply assume that state and civil society organisations differ, in that they have unequal access to state power, is one we need to move away from. Instead, we need to try and understand how capacities to act are produced, reduced and obliterated by both state bureaucrats and different civil society organisations that deploy certain tactics, strategies and models.

Our analytical and theoretical approach to the relations between state and civil society must often try to show the kaleidoscope of bureaucrats, practices of intervention and civil society group's strategies for coping with intervention by accommodating or resisting state intervention practices.

LOCAL KNOWLEDGE

The other important theoretical and conceptual problem sharply highlighted by the social drama above, is the issue of knowledge and how this process impacts on the process of development within the area of Bethelsdorp. Equally important is what meaning and interpretations local actors, including researchers and development activists, attach to the process of knowledge construction. Key to this process is the need for understanding the process of knowledge production and the reproduction and transformation thereof.

It is evident that the inhabitants of Bethelsdorp have a complex, yet interesting history that must be examined. Such a history has been constructed through years of activism and involvement in struggle by different social actors residing in the area.

This process of activism and struggle is further made evident in the language used by one of the key informants in the narrative above when he constantly refers to himself as an activist who was experienced in struggle. The actor further goes on to draw a contrasting interpretation between a former activist in government and an old apartheid bureaucrat in terms of consciousness.

Thus, the ex-ANC activist perceives himself to have, over the years, acquired a different form of knowledge to that of the National Party member who did not have such experience as he had formerly organically acquired that knowledge through a process of struggle and by working with local communities.

The National Party actor represents, to the ex-ANC activist, someone who has been placed in her position because she is perceived to have expert knowledge that the other actors do not posses.

'Knowledge is constituted by the ways in which people categorise, code, process and impute meaning to their experiences. This is as true of the "scientific"' as it is of the "non-scientific", everyday forms of knowledge. We should not, therefore, equate knowledge with some professional, specialised or esoteric set of data or ideas. It is something that everyone possesses, even though the grounds for belief and the procedures for validation of knowledge-claims will vary. Nor should the concept of knowledge carry with it the implication of "discovering the real facts", as if they lay "out there", ready for uncovering. Such a view is based upon objectivism, which assumes that the world is composed of facts and that the goal of knowledge is to provide a literal account of what the world is like '(Knor-Cetina 1981: 1-3).

Hence in this case, the drama reveals the meaning attached to knowledge construction and reproduction by certain actors within the Metro in the Eastern Cape Province. To them, knowledge represents some form of professional, specialised or esoteric set of data or ideas. This approach to knowledge construction and production poses different sets of problems for development processes at different levels of society. Of relevance in this case is their impact at a local level (micro level) for service delivery, capacity building and the livelihoods of local people.

My key argument, emerging from this drama, is that we should not make any ontological distinction between types of knowledge; for example, bureaucratic knowledge, expert knowledge and local knowledge. This also applies to the so-called scientific knowledge as opposed to everyday knowledge. Robert Chambers (1983) and Paul Richards (1985) make a similar argument and, according to them, the practical everyday knowledge of ordinary people can enrich science and improve development practice.

In my view, knowledge should be seen as a social construct and/or process[22] by which various social actors, through their different practical experiences, construct and deconstruct

---

22. For further elaborations on knowledge as a social process, see Box (1989: 167), where, through various case studies, he illustrates this point.

knowledge and thus through this process shape their everyday lives.

This view also implies that our approach to the construction of knowledge should not be an abstract or formalistic one. Rather, we should open the path to the re-evaluation of science in the making. Knowledge is not generated in abstract but in relation to the everyday contingencies and struggles that constitute social life.

'Furthermore, knowledge is not simply something that is possessed, accumulated and un-problematically imposed upon others (Foucault, in Gordon 1980). Nor can it be measured precisely in terms of some notion of quantity or quality. It emerges out of the process of social interaction and is essentially a joint product of the encounter and fusion of horizons. It must therefore, like power, be looked at relationally and not treated as if it could be depleted or used up.'

'That someone has power or knowledge does not entail that others are without. A zero-sum model is thus misplaced. Nevertheless, both power and knowledge may become reified in social life; that is, we often think of them as being real material things possessed by actors; and we turn to regard them as unquestioned "givens". This process of reification is, of course, an essential part of the ongoing struggles over meaning and control of strategic relationships and resources. Knowledge encounters involve the struggle between actors whereby certain of them attempt to enrol others in their "projects", getting them to accept certain frames of meaning and winning them over to their points of view. If they succeed, then other parties delegate power to them. These struggles focus around the fixing of key points that have a controlling influence over the exchanges and attributions of meaning (including the acceptance of reified notions such as authority)' (Long, 2001: 184).

Finally, the social drama reveals to us that politics and ideologies play a central role in influencing processes of project development.

CONCLUSION DISCUSSION

In this chapter I have tried to reconcile information contained in historical documents about development practices with the experiences and conceptualisations of a variety of local actors located in Bethelsdorp. Moreover, I give an account of the descriptions by local actors regarding how political conflicts located in colonial history had a wide influence on and affected their relationship with projects at a local level.

I argue that the current social development processes taking place within the Bethelsdorp area are affected by notions of deterministic, linear and externalist theoretical models of development.

Important variables such as equality, service delivery and capacity building are examined from the perspective of project development within the area of Bethelsdorp. It is evident that they are interwoven with the actual dynamics of project development and thus are not separated from this process. They are dynamically shaped by the different actors involved in the process of development within the area and thus cannot be measured or quantified.

The chapter provides us with a detailed account of the complex nature of conflict between state and civil society within the area of Bethelsdorp in the Eastern Cape of South Africa. Within this process I examined the different interfaces amongst the different social actors involved in the implementation of development projects in the area. I focus upon the interplay between different life worlds and bodies of knowledge and explore this from the point of view of the dilemmas faced by different individuals and groups of local actors like the local people of Bethelsdorp and their trust in their efforts to gain resources from the state for sustaining their projects. The efforts of the state (in the form of provincial and local government) as an intervening party to deal with complex development programmes at a local level is also examined.

In using the "interface" concept and the concept of the actor-oriented approach, I was able to identify and find the following key issues:

The complex nature of local development processes, within the Bethelsdorp area, which is driven by project development, involves different actors operating at different levels.

It is within this context that a vacuum exists between the two scales of macro and micro (that is, national and local). The interface between the two becomes crucial for understanding the development projects at a local level and the participation of local actors in the implementation of development projects.

This indicates that there are no direct and linear interrelations between macro goals and macro outcomes. The outcome of any development programmes (here the same applies to project development processes) is always mediated by the micro cosmoses through which it passes. Hence, knowledge and the dynamics of knowledge at a local level are essential to assessing the actual and/or potential impact at a local level.

The discussions in this chapter prove that the tendency by many development experts and planners of conceptualising the process as essentially linear in nature, is a gross simplification of a much more complicated set of processes that involve the reinterpretation of the goals of the project during the implementation process itself, such that there is in fact no straight line from programme to outcomes. This point is well illustrated in the social drama between the Bethelsdorp activist and the local government official narrated in this chapter. The claims of the activist that the state always wants to plan for the community without knowing what the community wants, indicates that the Bethelsdorp Development Trust and the local people it represents are affected by the linear notion of development paradigm.

During the period of the 1980s, with a growing recognition of the deficiencies of these models, a different and new paradigm began to emerge amongst development planners and policy experts. The dominant view that emerged amongst planners was that the process of development planning and project implementation should take the form of a transactional process involving negotiations over goals and means between parties with conflicting or diverging interests, and not simply an execution of a particular policy (Warwick, 1982). The findings of this chapter indicate that in the Eastern Cape Province of South Africa, and in particular within the area of Bethelsdorp, this particular theoretical paradigm still has not gained ground.

An important issue that can be observed from the Bethelsdorp case, is the role played by politics and ideologies in social development processes. The case clearly shows how ideologies and politics shape and influence the social behaviour of local actors involved in development processes and processes of project development. It also points to how, what are often seen as un-theoretical perceptions of those who are not experts can slow down the process of development transformation.

The case highlights the fact that knowledge, with its dynamics, is a socially negotiated process where different social actors construct knowledge and deconstruct knowledge and thus, through this process, shape development processes. In short, no one has a monopoly on knowledge.

What further emerges out of this Bethelsdorp case is that the processes of development and project management and implementation cannot be managed and planned as they are constantly shaped and re-shaped[23] through negotiations by individuals and groups involved in different everyday life struggles.

Finally, the challenge for development planners, researchers, policy implementers and activists involved in the South African development transitional process is that we are now at a critical

---

23. For a similar case, see Dikeni, 1996, where in a different context at the Kruger National Park similar findings emerged.

and exciting turning point in this process, when old orthodoxies have largely given way, or have at least provided room, for new modes of conceptualisations of the complexities and dynamics of social change and development. Sociologically, the South African transitional process is pregnant with potential for new forms of theorising and conceptualisation. The challenge for all of us is to think dynamically and not be trapped in theoretical orthodoxies. Indeed in line with Kuhn (1962), social theorising and conceptualisation is composed of not one form of a singular paradigm but is rather based on a multiplicity of paradigms.

REFERENCES

Bierschenk, Th. (1988) *Development Projects as Arenas of Negotiation for Strategic Groups; A Cease from Benin.* Sociologia Ruralis, Vol XXVII: 113-145

Bourdieu, P. (1977) *Outline of a Theory of Practice.* Cambridge: Cambridge University Press.

Box L. de la Rive (1989) *Knowledge Networks and Cultivators: Cassava in The Domican Republic in N. Long Encounters at the Interface: A Perspective on Social Discontinuities in Rural Development.* Wageningen Studies in Sociology, no. 27, Wageningen Agricultural University.

Chambers, R. (1983) *Rural Development: Putting the Last First.* London, Lagos and New York: Longman.

Crehan K. and A. Von Oppen (1988) *Understanding of Development; The Story of Development Projects in Zambia.* Sociologia Ruralis, XXVII; 146-160

Dikeni L. (1996) *Habitat and Struggle: The Case of the Kruger National Park in South Africa.* Wageningen Agricultural University, The Netherlands M.S.c Thesis.

Dikeni, L. (2007) *Regaining the Old Paradigm: The Debate over Civil Society and State.* Dibuho Journal: Intellectual Journal, Forthcoming.

Foucault, M. (1973) *The Order of Things.* New York: Vintage.

Gordon, C. (ed.) (1980) *Power Knowledge: Selected Interviews and Other Writings 1972-1977* by Michel Foucault. New York: Pantheon Press.

Knorr-Cetina, K. D. (1981) *The Manufacture of Knowledge: An Essay on the Constructivist and Contextual Nature Of Science.* Oxford: Pergamon Press.

Kuhn, T. S. (1962) *The Structure of Scientific Revolutions.* Chicago: University of Chicago Press

Long. N (ed.) 1989 *Encounters at the Interface. A Perspective on Social Discontinuities in Rural Development.* PUDOC, Agricultural University, Wageningen.

Long. N. (2001) *Development Sociology Actor Perspective.* Routledge London

Long, N. and A. Long (eds.) (1992) *Battle Fields of Knowledge.* Routledge London/ New York

Luckmann and Schutz, T. (1973) *The Structure of the Life World.* Evanston Illinois: North West University Press

Richards, P. (1985) *Indigenous Agricultural Revolution.* London Hutchinson

Schutz A. (1962) *The Problem of Social Reality.* The Hague: Nijhoff Publishers

Vanderdoes, M. and A. Arce (1994) *The Use of Narratives in Project Evaluation.* A Case from Ecuador. Paper Presented During the Workshop Mediating Sustainability, Wageningen Agricultural University, Department of Sociology of Rural Development.

Van Dusseldorp, D. (1993) *Projects for Rural Development in The Third World: Preparation and Implementation.* Lecture Notes Wageningen Agricultural University, Department of Sociology of Rural Development

Vries, P De (1992) *A Research Journey: On Actors Concepts and the Text* in: N. Long and A. Long (ed.) *Battle Fields of Knowledge: The Interlocking of Theory and Practice in Social Research and Development.* Routledge London/ New York

South African Development Perspectives In Question

CHAPTER 4

The Case of St. Lucia:
In KwaZulu-Natal

*Planned State Intervention Practices, Rural
Livelihoods, Actors' Perspectives and Interest in
Projects and Development*

INTRODUCTION

State intervention practices essentially refer to the ways and means of how the State and other parties intervene in the lives of its citizens. This covers formally organised state agencies and also the impact of other intervening parties, such as commercial companies and enterprises that attempt to control and organise production and the commercialisation of different products. We need to look at the issues that emerge in terms of the interaction between different local groups and the intervening actors and entities.

The findings of Chapter 2 indicate that the South African scientists and authors (including State practitioners) are trapped in theoretical models of the 60s and 70s that espouse a rather mechanical model of the relationship between policy, implementation and outcomes that imply some kind of step-by-step progression from policy implementation to outcomes.

In this chapter, using a case study on St. Lucia, a World Heritage Site, I show the reader how government agencies in the form of the Department of Social Development (DSD) of South Africa and the Department of Environment and Tourism (DEAT) are engaged in this form of developmental practice.

The chapter further shows how local groups in the area, who actively pursue their own development projects, clash with the interests of central authority and resort to various strategies, images and contestations to secure their livelihoods.

PLANNED INTERVENTION AT WORK: THE ST. LUCIA CASE

The broad objective of the study, which was carried out in collaboration with the department of Social Development (DSD) of South Africa, was to examine the interrelations between population, environment and development and how these interact (and counteract) with each other at a local level[24]. The problem holders were the Mtubatuba Local Municipality and the greater St Lucia Wetlands Park.

Though the study did not have a particular host, the Greater St Lucia Park (GSLWP) authorities and the local municipality of Mtubatuba can be regarded as such. In this area, population, environment and development issues are key dominating factors for the social development of the region at a local level. A key area of focus in the study is the "Greater St Lucia", a wetlands park (and the immediate Surrounding areas) that has been declared a World Heritage Site.

The environmental and developmental, objectives of the Mtubatuba Integrated Development Plan (IDP) review document (2003),[25] coincide with some of the objectives of this study. Some of the key developmental objectives of the IDP document are: (1) to ensure that developmental projects and proposals that are of benefit to, or directly impact upon, the municipal area and its communities are planned for, and managed, concurrently. (2) To ensure that the appropriate structures are put in place between the municipalities and its communities, adjacent municipalities, the district municipality

---

24. For an interesting and elaborated example (based on different narrative accounts) of how these some-times conflict with each other and lead to more social problems, see Dikeni (1996), where a detailed account of the complex nature of a conflict between "history", "people" and "space" is given on the problems between the Kruger National Park, the state, non-governmental organisations and the local people surrounding it.
25. The Mtubatuba Integrated Development Plan (IDP) review document (2003) is a report whose main purpose is to review whether and how the IDP strategic framework and the municipal priorities are being implemented, and whether they converge as a general trend.

and other statutory authorities and organisations in order to facilitate communication, cooperation and joint action planning, development and administration. Seen in this sense, the IDP document has become one key criteria used in this study to examine performance within the areas under study.

OVERALL OBJECTIVES

In 2003, I was appointed as a researcher by the South African Department of Social Development to conduct a study on the interaction between population, environment and development within the St Lucia Wetlands Park and to provide information to government and the business sector in relation to how government intervention policy is felt and socially interpreted on the ground. Key to this process was an assessment of public sector policies and resultant projects, initiatives and services on the lives of local people and/or communities, households and individuals.

In the study, issues such as employment creation, income generation, the impact of state policies on the community (local people) outreach and cost effectiveness were being used as the criteria for assessing the impact of state policy initiatives at a local level.

In the field, a wide range of broad and interrelated issues and questions served as the basis and focus of the study. These were:

✦ The profiling of the socio-demographic trends (of the area under study)
✦ The identification of government projects and initiatives implemented
✦ The establishment of the success of specific initiatives, in terms of declared goals and/or business plans
✦ Determining their impact, in relation to reversing unemployment trends, and also in relation to social and environmental impacts

- Assessing these impacts in their totality, and also in relation to key contexts such as poverty, education, health, local government and such specific concerns as land use
- Assess correctness of targeting, in relation to reported local needs, and in relation to special aspects of delivery
- Consider access and communication for such interventions, in an institutional context: What local institutions are able to articulate service demands and shortfalls to local and national government? Are designated formal institutions responsive? What other institutions exist and are in contact? With which departments are they in contact?
- Make the best possible trend assessments of delivery at the local level: has delivery been improving, deteriorating or showing mixed results across the range of services and benefits under consideration? How far has the delivery process met its own objectives in the local context and what are the reported reasons?

Analysis

Evidently, the point made in earlier chapters on the conceptualisation of planned development in-terms of the relationship between policy, implementation and outcome is made clear here by the objectives of the state in evaluating its development programmes within the area. The linearity, mechanical approach and prescriptive nature of this process can be clearly observed from the objectives of the study. Hence, as the following sections in this chapter will show, in my attempts to accommodate government objectives and interests, I also adopted the theoretical framework of the actor-oriented approach and through this approach was able to delineate the various social practices of the actors involved in development processes within the area.

ANALYTICAL FRAMEWORK

The study seeks to approach these issues and questions from the point of view of different social actors (stakeholders) located in different areas of St Lucia, Mtubatuba and Dukuduku in the KwaZulu-Natal province (KZN).

The central argument being that different social actors in the areas under study, will place different significance on population, development and environmental issues and will therefore have different priorities for policy formulation and implementation. This is so, because it is assumed in this study that there are three key elements to be considered in any developmental policy process:

✦ First, there must be consensus that the status quo is unacceptable;

✦ Second, trade-offs between alternative policies must be acknowledged and policy options developed; and

✦ Third, a political process needs to be initiated that will allow viable policies for the future.

The study identifies social actors according to their relationship to the direct use of the resource, and distinguishes four major groups: the direct users themselves (e.g. local communities and/or parks board), regulators of the use of affected areas (e.g. local municipal), service providers (e.g. local business etc.) and representatives (e.g. community and/or civil society organisations).

The key argument of the study is that a process of policy elaboration based on demands made at a local level must focus on strengthening the linkages between the direct users themselves and policy organisations both within government and civil society and on the relationship between the two.[26]

As with the previous chapters, the theoretical framework adopted in this chapter is that of the actor-oriented approach, conceptualised as a social interface. Special care is taken to

---

26. For an interesting example of this approach see Dikeni, Moorehead and Schoones (1996).

ensure that the importance of actors who do not directly act at the level of the interface is not neglected or underestimated. For the purposes of this study, I will accommodate some of these problems and develop an appropriate approach for analysing complex problems of environment, development and population.

POPULATION, DEVELOPMENT AND THE ENVIRONMENT: ACTORS' PERSPECTIVES AND INTERESTS

The Local Business People: SDI, Craft Workers and the Timber Industry

Business people aim to make profits from their various small, medium and large enterprises. In the case of the area under study, this means the Spatial Development Initiatives (SDIs), the local craftspeople, the timber industry and other small retailers located in both Mtubatuba and the Greater St Lucia Wetlands Park area.

This section of the chapter will focus mainly on the Spatial Development Initiatives (SDIs), the local craftspeople and the timber industry, as these dominate the sector within the case study area.

The Spatial Development Initiatives (SDIs)

Realising the need for establishing export-oriented zones and the need for encouraging foreign direct investment, the South African government, through its Department of Trade and Industry (DTI), established twelve Spatial Development Initiatives (SDIs) across the country and parts of Southern Africa.

Some of the key objectives of the Spatial Development Initiatives (SDIs) were to improve and raise the socio-economic status of geographic areas (in South Africa and Southern Africa) that have enormous economic potential but have been historically underutilised and underdeveloped. Key to their economic strategy was to improve and raise the socio-economic status of these areas by removing constraints to economic growth in affected areas. To do this means that Spatial Development Initiatives (SDIs) themselves must be attractive to local and international investors so that they can become preferred destinations for investment. Hence, they were charged with the task of identifying constraints and implementing corrective programs within their respective areas.

Weak infrastructure and an enabling regulatory framework had been identified as key barriers to investment. It has been argued that Spatial Development Initiatives (SDIs) 'have implemented programmes that have addressed these barriers within a developmental framework, and ensuring that local communities reap the maximum benefits from these programmes and future investments....' (unpublished IDP document)

The most relevant Spatial Development Initiatives (SDIs) for the area under study were the Richards Bay Empangeni SDIs and the Lubombo SDI. This is so because of their closeness in proximity to the Greater St Lucia Wetlands Park (GSLWP) and the relevant developmental, economical and environmental objectives espoused by the two SDIs for the Greater St Lucia Wetlands Park geographical space.

The Lubombo Spatial Development Initiative forms part of the twelve SDIs initiated by the South African government (including three other governments in Southern Africa) and its relevant department, the Department of Trade and Industry (DTI). In South Africa it is located in the Northern part of the KwaZulu-Natal (KZN) province. Key to some of its aims and objectives at a regional level, is the generation of economic growth by making maximum use of the inherent but underutilised potential of the area.

The aim is to ensure that governments maximise private sector involvement; to create an attractive and stable environment for investors to operate in; to maximise job creation by ensuring that the new industries being stimulated are competitive and have a long-term future in the region; to create broader ownership patterns in the regional economy by creating new small businesses and encouraging outside investors to form joint ventures with local entrepreneurs and communities, and to ensure cooperation between all levels of government within the Southern African region involved in Spatial Development work.

Key to some of the economic activities supported and encouraged by the Lubombo SDI at the regional level, are tourism, agri-business and building construction, et al.

In South Africa, and especially in the KwaZulu-Natal (KZN) province, the Greater St Lucia Wetlands Park (GSLWP) is the most direct macro-economic initiative and/or intervention mechanism of the SDI. It is the anchor tourism project that has been designed to attract large-scale investments. It is aiming at establishing itself as a major national and international tourist destination within the country and the region.

The Greater St Lucia Wetlands Park is structured and managed by three agencies that have a direct impact on its operational activities. These are: KwaZulu-Natal Wildlife, which is responsible for managing the conservation regulations; the KwaZulu-Natal Economic Council, which is responsible for managing direct investment within the area, and the Social, Environment and Development section, which is mainly responsible for promoting the broader development goals of the Lubombo Spatial Development Initiative.

Amongst these three agencies, it can arguably be said that the Social, Environment and Development section as an agency is better placed to socially interface, intervene and act with different forms of agencies with a direct interest in the Greater St Lucia Wetlands Park area (GSLWP). This is so, because of both its tasks, sub-tasks and set goals, which are to structure sustainable partnerships between the community (local people), business people, the government and environmental authorities. Some of its stated goals are:

✦ Members of the target community should have ownership or equity interests in the productive assets of the Greater St Lucia Wetlands Park (GSLWP). This involves the incorporation of communal land into the productive economy of the Park, as well as equity participation by the target community in the commercial enterprises of the Greater St Lucia Wetlands Park (GSLWP)

✦ The target community should have management participation in the core activities of the park. This involves the training and appointment of members of the target communities at all management levels of the Park authority, as well as in the commercial enterprises established in the Greater St Lucia Wetlands Park (GSLWP).

✦ There should be secondary enterprise linkages between economic activities of the Park and suppliers of goods and services from the target community. This will involve developing and implementing appropriate procurement and SMME support policies in close coordination with other support agencies, including local government.

Seen in this sense, it can be argued that the Lubombo SDI should have a great social, environmental, economic and developmental impact on the Great St Lucia Wetlands Park (GSLWP) and its surrounding areas. The following sections will further substantiate this view.

Craft Workers

Craft workers are in themselves service providers and small businesses at the same time. At a broader regional level they supposedly have institutional support from the Greater St Lucia Wetlands Park (GSLWP) authorities. According to one of the local informants, there were (during the time the study was conducted) two programmes in operation designed to help craft workers in the GSLWP. These are the Greater St Lucia Wetlands Park (GSLWP) Cultural programme and the GSLWP Craft Programme.

The latter is meant to support and develop local culture by using cultural activities to support economic, cultural and social development programmes. In the area under study, these reside in and around the surrounding areas of the greater St Lucia Wetlands Park (GSLWP) in Dukuduku, Khula Village and Kwamsane, where the people can often be found on the roadsides selling various crafts, fruits and vegetables to both local residents and tourists.

The residents' main income derives from growing fruit, which they in turn sell in different local markets, and from cutting trees from the forests, which they use for making curios to sell at the local markets.

According to most of the crafters interviewed in the area the production and sale of crafts are crucial to their livelihood strategies. One of the informants said:

> ... The problem many of us in the surrounding areas like Dukuduku and Khula Village face is that some of us are educated and some of us are uneducated ... But we all need jobs, and jobs are scarce in these areas. Those who are lucky have to travel from Dukuduku and Khula Village to Richards Bay to find work ... Those who are not lucky just have to find other alternatives to survive ... This is what I have chosen... [crafting] (**Fieldwork Notes, 2003**).

Despite the meager incomes received through the craft industry by most crafters, for those of them interviewed, the industry is perceived as complex and is open to abuse by various social actors operating within it. This is so because incomes received through crafting activities are unequally distributed between producers and sellers. Producers earn far less than traders do. As one of the young Crafters said:

> ... *You see, I prefer to make my own curios and sell them on the roadside as opposed to asking someone to sell them at the market in St Lucia ... because in this work [industry] ... we are robbing each other and are robbed at the same time. A shop owner buys from me and sells my curios for a more profitable price in the shop ... the same happens with me when perhaps asking a friend at the market to do it for me ... Instead of all this, I could sell my own things and get them sold quickly and make money...* **(Fieldwork Notes, 2003).**

Linked to these social problems and concerns are many other general problems (important for the livelihoods of the crafters) that were cited by the crafters living in and around the surrounding areas of the Greater St Lucia Wetlands Park (GSLWP). These vary and impact on each other. Some of them are:

✦ Transport and communication: Most crafters from Dukuduku and Khula Village complained about the lack of transport infrastructure for transporting their crafts from their respective areas to the main market in St Lucia.

✦ Almost all the crafters interviewed complained about the need for easy access to raw materials. According to them, it is very difficult to get good-quality raw materials from their areas of residence. This results in them not producing quality products.

✦ Some crafters raised the issue of rising crime within the St Lucia market. Most of them claimed that they do not have proper storage facilities for their goods. According to them this results in local buyers stealing their curios at night when they are not around.

✦ Almost all crafters complained about the smallness of space allocated to them at the St Lucia market. Linked to this problem, they claim, is the lack of shelters on the roadsides.

✦ According to most crafters, international tourists are not buying much of their goods.

✦ The issue of marketing and selling their goods was another very important issue for almost all the crafters interviewed. For this, they suggested that the state support them by providing them with the necessary skills required.

The Timber Industry and the Forests:

The key objectives of the timber industry are to supply timber for paper mills and through this make a profit.[27] To do this meant that timber companies operating in the area had to buy up farms, which had previously engaged in agricultural practices, during the1990s and 2000s and transform them into large timber estates. This also meant, establishing "wood lots" in communally-owned tribal land near the St Lucia Wetlands area.

Discussions with the timber industry workers indicated that this resulted in a direct land conflict with both agricultural producers and local communities (local residence) in the area. As one industry member explains:

> ... *I really do not know how people expect us to survive; we are business people, our aim, as with any other business people, is to make money! However, we are also providing services to the country... If we were not here, believe me, there would be no books for children in the schools, no boxes to pack goods for export purposes and no jobs for the local black folks... You see*

27. Discussions with local people indicate that timber industries used to be the main providers of jobs in the area under study. Included amongst people employed by the industry are illegal migrants from neighbouring countries such as Mozambique.

Mr. Dikeni, what we have here is that the guy who, say for example, sells mangoes or avocados to the local people, that is 'mos' his market and he must produce for it.

… And now the guy needs enough land for growing his product, he goes to the parks board and the local municipality and talks about us [Timber Industry producers] bad… bad…bad… They want to make money, we also want to make money… And now on the other hand you have these local blacks with no jobs, coming from the black township and wanting jobs. They do not know that we are creating jobs for them through our industry. They listen to these agricultural producers and environmentalisst, the green guys who are telling them we are wrong… They get money from these guys…! I am telling you… Government must come and sort out this mess before it's too late…! (**Fieldwork notes, 2003**).

Various people in the timber industry argued that the best way to intervene in resolving this land conflict is by ensuring that the existing land reform process, implemented by the state, takes the form of an economic unit. In short, this implies that land should be allocated in units large enough to provide livelihoods for emergent farmers, who will then be able to repay any loans from the revenue the farm makes.

The current land reform process initiatives also led to the displacement of many farmworkers, including the rural poor living in the area. On an environmental level, this meant increased pressure on the environment and an increase in environmental destruction.

Although it is difficult to assess the environmental degradation impact of the timber industry, discussions with people working in the forests indicate that, as wetlands dry out, the wetlands species become locally extinct, and it is quite possible that species that haven't previously been recorded, are being lost without ever having been discovered.

Linked to this, is the tendency of plantations in the area to spread from where they were originally planted, or to sporadically reappear in areas where they had been discontinued.[28] According to forest workers, this has had a devastating environmental effect on the forest of the area under study. As one forest worker explained:

> ... *We are really in trouble in terms of monitoring and documenting the different old species in the area. There is no mechanism for recording old indigenous species within the Richards Bay area that I know of... to the extent that, I do not think we know very well what is home-grown and what is alien. We kill what we know are alien species here today and in a few weeks they reappear elsewhere, these things just grow and grow non-stop. I do not want to complain... but this is a lot of work and it really hurts the soil...* (**Fieldwork Notes, 2003**).

However, despite these social problems the state has, in various ways, tried to intervene and change the situation. One of the intervention practices used by the state is an ongoing campaign to eradicate alien trees in the areas affected.

This meant, amongst other things, using herbicide sprays and other chemical applications. A critical issue for most foresters is not knowing what the effects of the use of these chemicals on the native species could be.

Some form of criticism on the management techniques used by the state can be found from foresters, who argue that the state methods and techniques are failing due to a lack of proper monitoring and ongoing follow-up.

Most people working in the forests however, claim that damage has already been done in sensitive catchment areas, which cannot be reversed.

---

27. Though difficult to give an exact figure of the area occupied by timber industries within the area under study, most workers indicated this to be the size of more than an economic unit. They however, argued that this varied from one area to another.

THE LOCAL COMMUNITIES (LOCAL RESIDENCE)

Local people (local communities) are different from most of the other groups described above in that they do not own much land and are a combination of different social actors (individuals and groups) making their livelihoods by crafting, selling fruit and vegetables and working in and outside the areas surrounding the Greater St Lucia Wetlands Park (GSLWP). Some also survive through farming small patches of land. This group raises livestock and attempts to cultivate crops — sometimes successfully and sometimes unsuccessfully.[29]

Dukuduku, Khula Village and Kwamsane are the three main local areas surrounding the greater St Lucia Wetlands Park. Mtubatuba, the local municipal area, is what the locals refer to as the local town.

The dominating issues emerging from this sector are social demands for various livelihood purposes. These are many, and are often conflictive and have a direct impact on the Greater St Lucia Wetlands Park (GSLWP). They include demands for jobs, better housing, better health facilities and land. The land issue is the most conflictive issue and has direct political, social and economic impacts on the Greater St Lucia Wetlands Park (GSLWP). As illustrated by this key informant on the area:

... You see (wabona), Leslie ... The problem here started in 1993 with the resettlement of our people from Dukuduku, which was then declared a State indigenous coastal forest to an alternative piece of land ... Which is today known as Khula Agricultural Village.[30] This happened after a long struggle between the community and the State. The community claimed that it was

29. Members of the farming group amongst the local people interviewed, were clear about one thing, and that is that the areas they were presently using for stocking were inadequate. In addition to this, they complained about a lack of access to credit and finance facilities. According to them, it was impossible to survive through raising livestock only and that they had to mix this with other diverse forms of off-farm activities such as working outside their areas of residence and selling fruit on the local markets.
30. Elsewhere, it is estimated that about 30 000 people settled in the Dukuduku forest during the period 1990–2000.

forcefully removed from its land and the State claimed that it was land to be used for conservation purposes. This resulted in the so-called illegal occupation of the Dukuduku forest by people. This in turn, resulted in the arrest of local people of the area… After some time negotiations took place, and a decision was taken by both the State and the local people to release those who were arrested … The community was then given a choice to choose a piece of land … Some people led by a certain Mr. Caiphus Sikhisela Mkhwanazi, a prince of the Mkhwananzi tribe moved to a piece of land where the Khula Village is now established … Some people refused to move and are still resident in the Dukuduku Forest … OK. Now, I hear that the municipality with some members of the community are trying to organise us to move to a different place called Zwelisha… [*my own translation*] (**Fieldwork notes 2003**).

Farmworkers

Distinct from — but closely connected to — the local communities sector are the farm workers living on farms surrounding the Greater St Lucia Wetlands Park. They are distinct, because unlike local people (local communities) they do not own land of their own.[31] However, they are connected to local people through kinship ties and other social relations. The land the farmworkers use is the farm of the landowners and the management of land is subject to the landowner's (their employers') priorities.

Most farmworkers interviewed expressed the wish to own their own houses. Farmworkers living around the Greater St Lucia Wetlands Park are some of the poorest people in the area, with low levels of formal education, low incomes and reduced access to both healthcare and transport facilities. They can often

---

31. Discussions with farmworkers about the land problem in the area indicated that those who required land wanted a small (an area the size of the Africa Centre) piece of land to plough. This, they argued, would help them to increase their livelihoods.

be found on the roadside asking for a lift. As one male farmworker we found on the roadside asking for a lift, explained to us:

> ... *Siyabonga ...Thank you for the lift. I do not know what I would have done if you guys did not turn up. You see, sometimes the bosses (abelungu) do not understand our problems regarding transport within the different areas. They give us holidays and expect us to go home and come back to work; without considering that we do not have transport... Mtubatuba where the rest of my family reside, is very far from where I work and despite the taxis being expensive, there are not many taxis going to where I work, this makes it difficult for us to travel and move long distances... And I cannot stay in the farm for the whole year without seeing my family members... Instead of giving us our own houses for us to live in so that our families can visit us or organising transport for us, these people make us stay in their little rooms in the farm and put restrictions on us. This makes it difficult for family members or even friends to visit... Well, what else can we do, a job is a job...* (My own translation) (**Fieldwork notes, 2003**).

Due to their marginal situation, farmworkers living in the area are not interested in grazing land, and environmental management is far down the list of their priorities. Their key issues relate to wages, housing and better health care facilities.

Another farmworker interviewed supports the views expressed by the roadside farmworker we encountered earlier on and further expressed his views in the following way:

> ... *I am from Dukuduku and my other two colleagues are from Kwamsane and Khula Village. We do not earn a lot of money; we do not own land and thus, have no interest in farming. But we are worried... spending your whole life in a farm and working for a farm owner without your own house is always an*

issue of concern for all of us. I hear government and some bosses saying we must be concerned about the trees and not cut them down... We must take care about the environment (Invelo) and protect it. Tell me... what about us, do they ever think about us? They should instead give us some land so that we can build our own houses and grow our own vegetables. It does not matter even if this piece of land could be as big as the Africa Centre... Where we sometimes go for meetings... (**Fieldwork Notes, 2003**).

Very little organisation exists within this group and they are in a very weak economic position. They have minimal interaction with the Parks Board authorities and other outside organisations. However, there are organisations from outside the area doing research and monitoring the lives of farmworkers (for example, the farmworkers' research). Organisations monitoring farmworkers' social lives that the researcher spoke to, argued very strongly that farmworkers should be given access to land and be provided with the required transport. However, this group has very little knowledge and influence at a policy level.

THE PARKS BOARD (PROTECTED AREA MANAGERS)

The key objectives of managers of protected areas, such as National Parks, are to: conserve biodiversity, act as stewards of national and international heritage, maintain protected areas as reservoirs of wildlife and protect the option values of wildlife and biodiversity for future generations. They also endeavor to increase the awareness of the public of conservation through tourism, educational programmes and the media. The Greater St Lucia Wetlands Park (GSLWP) Board is one of these protected area spaces.

Protected area managers are also service providers and have

developed sophisticated technologies for the management of their boundaries. They are increasingly providing tourism facilities and environmental education programmes targeting the young. However, their approach is often heavily top-down in terms of their relationship to local people and they have very limited capacity to deal with participatory wildlife management issues in partnership with communities.

National Parks and other protected areas have very strong linkages with the tourism industry, environmental NGOs, the Parks boards and international wildlife and conservation organisations. They identify strongly with international conventions for the protection of species, and believe the resources they manage are of global importance; thus the broader national and international community are among the important social actors in the conservation of protected areas.

Protected area managers argue that parks and other conservation zones should be as large as possible and run as one integrated unit. They are increasingly aware of the need to share some of the benefits of protected area management with local people, although they insist that the management of these areas remains with protected area authorities. In following this policy, they provide some employment opportunities for local people, and some benefits for local people surrounding protected areas, such as ecotourism and handycraft production. The Greater St Lucia Wetlands Park (GSLWP) espoused some of these macro objectives and has incorporated them within its programmes.

At a regional (and/or meso) level, through the broad SDI programme for the region, and specifically for the area under study, it has initiated project-related programmes. These are, as communicated by one of the informants working in the Parks board:

... There is not much happening here in terms of local community development. The emphasis is on biodiversity, conservation and ecotourism ... There are only three main

community development projects initiated here. These are a community levy, an environmental education programme and a cultural tourism programme... All of them are administered by Ezemvelo KwaZulu-Natal Wildlife (EKZN) ... They are responsible for managing biodiversity conservation for the GSLWP and the generation of funds from tourists who use their tourism facilities ... These three programmes, are used for the development of surrounding areas such as Dukuduku and Khula Agricultural Village. They include:

✦ *Cultural Tourism Programme: The main objective of which is to promote good neighborhood relations with Khula Village and the other villages ... The Parks Board, Ezemvelo KwaZulu-Natal Wildlife trained some people from the Khula Village in ways of doing ecotourism. The Wildlife Trust was also involved, through a programme they are running that trains tour guides... As a result of these initiatives one of the community members, residing at Khula Village, initiated his own programme, which is partially operating and is known as Veyane Cultural Village... The Veyane Cultural Village is owned by Mr. Philip Mkhwanazi and is situated at the entrance of Khula Village ... You must go and see it ... It enjoys visits by both domestic and international tourists. The Veyane Cultural Village offers various forms of activities such as Zulu dancing and cultural music. It also serves as a tour-operating company offering guided tours to tourists who want to see wildlife in and around the Greater St Lucia Wetlands Park ...*

✦ *Community Levy Fund... The Community Levy Fund is responsible for managing biodiversity conservation for the Greater St Lucia Wetlands Park and the province. More specifically ... they generate money for the Khula Agricultural Village; these funds are generated at the Crocodile Centre and the St Lucia reservation office, which administers two campsites and a cruise boat known as Santa Lucia. Projects*

*that the programme has implemented thus far are, at Khula
Village... (1) A craft market called Siyabonga... (2)
Laboratories at Silethukukhanya high school worth R125,000
(3) A proposal for about R224,000 is also being submitted for
building a community hall...*

Response: Thousand

✦ *The Environmental Education Programme ... : For this
programme we can count the following programmes that focus
mainly on educational biodiversity (I) School programmes ...
Where a community conservation officer would visit schools to
present lessons on various topics relevant to the school
curriculum ... (II) Teachers workshops on various topics such as
Ecosystems, Estuarine Ecology, Marine Environment, etc. (III)
The formation of environmental clubs (IV) Reserved field visits
... That is, conducting field excursions for learners and
educators ... (V) Finally, the programme-protected area
neighbours ... Where various presentations are made at liaison
forum meetings ...* (**Fieldwork notes, 2003**).

The Beach Action Committee and the 4x4 Issue

Another issue faced by the protected area managers is what is
commonly known as the 4x4 issue. In short, the 4x4 issue was an
intervention regulatory mechanism, used by the National
Department of Environmental Affairs and tourism (DEAT) to
regulate the use of 4x4s on all the local Beaches by banning them
from the beaches.

This created conflict between the different social groups and
the local authorities who are the enforcers of the ban. While the
interest groups argued strongly that the ban has an effect on
their local economy; the State (through the local authorities)
argued that the use of 4x4s has a negative effect on the
environment.

This resulted in the formation of an action group and/or pressure group, by the local business people residing in the area of St Lucia, called the Beach Action Committee consisting of various business people. It sees its main task as campaigning against the ban through lobbying various groups of influential people such as politicians and local residents living in and around St Lucia.

On this issue, different social actors attach different meanings and give different interpretations on the ban. Some actors are in favor of the ban by the state and some are against the ban. Other actors interviewed (especially some members of the Parks Board), argued very strongly that there was no need for a ban on all beaches. They argued that on some beaches the ban should have been allowed while on others it should not have been allowed.

They also suggested that a scientific study should be conducted to investigate the effects and/or impacts of 4x4s on the beaches. This continues to be an issue of attention and debate for local people in the area.

FINDINGS AND ANALYSIS

The following is a summary of key findings based on an interpretation of different forms of narratives, data, interviews and observations in the field.

An attempt is being made here to summarise a complex set of findings, based on the interpretations and conceptualisations of a variety of local actors with regard to the issue of population, environment, and development in the Greater St Lucia Wetlands Park (GSLWP).

In this section, information contained in different texts on the important issue of population, environment and development is reconciled with a variety of local actors' views and perspectives

---

32. Here the concept of "multiple realities" as used by Schutz and Luckmann (1962) and Luckmann and Schutz (1973) is used to describe how different actors accord different interpretations to the same situations or events, and thus construct differing social realities.

so as to reach some consensus.[32] Through the use of the concept of the actor-oriented approach and interface analyses I was able to analyse and find the following:

Interpretation, Interests and Livelihoods

✦ Land-reform approaches need to consider a wider range of property types, and expand beyond the current focus on the reallocation of private property in smaller units.

✦ Communities surrounding St Lucia (a protected area) should have the opportunity to benefit from such resources and be represented on the management of such bodies.

✦ The existing interpretation (amongst different social actors interviewed) of the economic unit is redundant and needs to be replaced by a much broader concept of a livelihood unit that recognises people's diverse livelihood activities.

✦ The Lubombo Spatial Development Initiative (SDIs) project[33,] while being a good macro-economic initiative with good intentions, largely benefits big business and has not yet been fully understood and/or internalised by local people in areas such as Kwamsane, Dukuduku, Khula Village and other villages in the area. This is so because of the high levels of unemployment and illiteracy within the area. It can also be argued that government communication strategy at a local level has failed to inform local people about this project initiative.

✦ Conservation and commercial practices should generate direct benefits for the surrounding communities and local people in the short, medium and long terms.

✦ The environmental integrity of the areas under study must not be compromised by economic activity.

✦ The use of universal planning norms, such as the ban of 4x4 on the beach by the National Department of

---

33. In line with others, for example (Bierschenk, 1988, Crehan and Van Oppen 1988, Van Dusseldorp 1993), projects in this study are conceptualised as arenas of struggle for scarce resources.

Environmental Affairs and Tourism (DEAT) and the continuing conflict (and/or tension) between state authorities and local people in the Dukuduku forest, do not make sense. There is a need to move towards more local level planning, involving much more discussion with local land users and a more participative approach to planning that recognises the livelihood requirements of different people.

State Intervention at a Local Level

The role of local government departments in broader environmental regulation and control functions remains an area of debate and disagreement amongst different social actors. For example, at present there is a conflicting debate taking place amongst all stakeholders on the banning of 4x4s from the beach by the state. On this issue, different social actors have a different response towards the ban:

The local municipality and the Parks Board serve as regulators and legally enforce the ban. Other social actors like the local people and small business respond to the issue based on their interests. The State, at a local level, clearly has an interventionist role to play in this conflict. However, different social actors like the small businesses are still contesting this role — which poses difficulties for the State, in terms of playing its role of regulation and control at a local level.

There is also a strong finding emerging from the officials working in the Parks Board and in the different camps surrounding St Lucia. According to them, the ban does not differentiate between different camps and their objectives (i.e. some camps may accommodate 4x4s and some may not be able to accommodate them).

Exploring ways in which cross-sectoral concerns are incorporated into state policy is an ongoing challenge and is critical, requiring innovative and creative solutions.

More Information Needed

During the fieldwork process different forms of discussions took place with different social actors within and outside government. One issue of importance that emerged out of these debates was the identification of three key areas where investment in focused research would help illuminate some important policy dilemmas faced by the state within the different areas under study. They are:

Comparative advantage of land use options:
An appraisal of the full economic value of different land use system is required for the different areas under study.

Forestry and degradation
On the forestry level, a difficulty caused by the poor understanding of biological and economic understanding of degradation processes (by the researcher) means that further research needs to be conducted with regards to this if policy is to offer any useful direction on the trade-off between current production and future sustainability.

Local people and their livelihood strategies
Currently there is very little understanding of the impact of 4x4s on the beaches (and/or there are different conflicting statements) and how this in turn affects the rural poor.

Linked to this problem is limited data and/or information on the composition of rural livelihoods by the rural poor of the area under study. To address this problem new research will need to be carried out based on comparative case study material across a diversity of land-use sites taking into account that the process of land-use in the area is dynamic and frequently changing. This also implies an understanding of the diverse activities in the use of land that make up rural livelihoods.

The issue of the HIV / AIDS pandemic (and other diseases like TB and malaria) is often cited as an issue affecting local people, in particular young adults and the local industry. In short, the disease has an effect on the local economy in the area. Further research will have to be done with regards to the exact economic impact of the disease on local people.

Finally, a complex problem for local residents is the issue of crafts and ecotourism. Most people interviewed cited the importance of this for their livelihoods. However, various conflicting claims were made with regards to the decline of local tourists in the area, which has an impact on the craft market.

Different problems regarding the marketing facilities provided were also raised as key negative factors for the craft producers. These are: the allocation of space, the areas allocated for selling craft, local crime and other problems. Linked to all of these problems was the problem of financial skills in costing and managing their crafts.

A key problem cited by some tourists (during informal discussions) with regards to the industry was the transportation of these goods. Most of the tourists claimed that luggage weight restrictions at the airports limit the amount of goods they can travel with. Which suggests that the state at different levels would need to examine means and ways of how both domestic and international tourists can have better means of transporting their goods.

Planned Intervention

Contrary to other research studies done (which often place a pre-set focus on the issue) on the HIV and AIDS pandemic, the issue in this study is treated as an emergent property, emerging from the broad objectives of the study. The issue here emerged

---

34. Despite statistical data provided by the Africa Centre on the number of people affected by the pandemic (in terms of numbers of deaths) in the area under study, it was very difficult to find local informants willing to disclose information on the effects of the disease on them in other ways.

from a variety of social actors interviewed in the field,[34] within the major theme and focus of the study on Population, Environment and Development using the case of St Lucia in KwaZulu-Natal.[35]

One of the key issues that was supposed to be examined in the field was the impact of public sector policies on the lives of local people. Issues such as employment creation, income generation, the impact of State policies on the State, outreach and cost effectiveness were being used as criteria for assessing the impact of State policy at a micro level.

The HIV and AIDS issue emerged out of these issues as one of the key issues affecting almost all different social actors interviewed in the field. It affects them in many different ways and cuts across different sectors of the local population.

For local people, living in and around the Greater St Lucia Wetlands Park (GSLWP), the key issue is often losing a family member who is a breadwinner for the family. According to the Africa Centre, which is responsible for research on HIV and AIDS in the area under study, the notable victims are young adults already working and/or beginning to work.

Crafters who also reside in local areas had similar problems. To them an issue of concern was the use of some of their female members (in particular those working on the roadside) as sex workers.

The key issue for the Timber industry is the loss of skilled workers who have gained their skills in various social ways, either through formal means and/or informal means (years of work experience and/or formal training). Truck drivers (due to their job, which often involves long hours of travelling on the road) were notably the most affected in the sector.

Though it is very difficult to obtain exact figures, the same findings seem to have emerged for the other industries and sectors in the area.

---

35. For more information on the various forms of actions and strategies employed by government, non-governmental organisations (NGOS) and the private sector in the area under study, see, for example, *Documenting Aids Case Studies in South Africa*, 2002.

Brief Discussion

In a brief and limited way this study has highlighted how, in many ways, the issues of population, environment and development interact and counteract with each other within the Greater St Lucia Wetlands Park (GLSWP) and the surrounding areas of Mtubatuba, Kwamsane, Khula Village and Dukuduku.

Evidently, different social groups and/or individuals, different social issues affecting different people in different ways, different social interests, different histories and different conditions require that different policy intervention methods would have to be used in mediating the many different social conflicts in the area. The State is placed in a better place to do this.

However, one key issue seems to be emerging (as an emerging property from the objectives of the study) and that is the issue of HIV and AIDS and its effects on the different social actors in the area. This issue cuts across a range of sectors and has specific effects on different actors.

Theoretical Analysis

Intervention Practices

The foregoing analysis and findings requires a theoretical and conceptual analysis that will connect both theory and practice. My starting point is that a critical analysis of policy intervention processes requires demythologising notions of planned development. That is, it is important to challenge the time/space definitions, normative assumptions and praxeology implied in orthodox intervention models, and to expose the limitations of certain theoretical conceptions that underpin them, paying particular attention to the theorisation of commoditisation, institutional corporation and the interrelations of state and civil society. This chapter offers such a critique and proposes as an alternative that we view intervention as a multiple reality made up of differing cultural perceptions and social interests, and constituted by the ongoing social and political struggles that take place between the various social actors involved (Long, 2001).

Hence, the need for us to deconstruct the concept of intervention and recognise it for what it fundamentally is, namely an ongoing, socially constructed and negotiated process and not simply the execution of an already-specified plan of action with expected outcomes as the analysis findings in the chapter indicate.

Rural Livelihoods

'Livelihood best expresses the idea of individuals and groups striving to make a living, attempting to meet their various consumption and economic necessities, coping with uncertainties, responding to new opportunities and choosing between different value positions. Studying livelihoods also entails identifying the relevant social units and fields of activity: one should not prejudge the issue, as many studies do, by fixing upon the more anchorage points for an analysis of economic life such as the household, the local community, the production sector or commodity chain. Indeed, in many situations, confederations of households and wide-ranging interpersonal networks embracing a wide variety of activities and cross-cutting so-called rural and urban contexts, as well as national frontiers, constitute the social fabric upon which livelihoods and commodity are woven. In addition, we need to take account of the normative and cultural dimensions of livelihoods, that is we need to explore the issue of lifestyles and the factors that shape them' (Long, 2001, P,11).

Wallman (1984) contributed to the debate on the theoretical conceptualisation of livelihoods by stating that livelihood is never just a matter of finding or making shelter, transacting money, getting food to put on the family table or to exchange on the market place. It is equally a matter of ownership and circulation of information, the management of skills and relationships and the affirmation of personal significance (involving issues of self-esteem) and group identity. The task of meeting obligations of security, identity and status, and organising time are as crucial to livelihood as bread and shelter.

Projects and Development

Projects may be conceived either as sets of interrelated and coordinated activities towards the achievements of specific goals according to a specific plan, or as social events and arenas of struggles between various social groups and actors with different life worlds and interests (Crehan and Oppen, 1988).

However, to only conceive projects primarily as a set of activities is not enough and can rather be limited. As Padopolous in his study of the Greek bureaucracy of the responsibilities and orbits at the interface between a rural bureaucracy and dynamic farmers shows and further elaborates:

'Although my definition of a "project" is much closer to the latter than the former conception of it for the research purposes of this thesis, the project is not conceived primarily as a set of activities, or as arenas of struggles, but it is defined as a bundle of responsibilities. Every actor's project is constituted by a set of specific and substantive responsibilities which — and this is a central assumption of the thesis — have to be allocated to certain actors if the project is to be implemented. During the negotiation process each actor attempts to allocate a specific responsibility of his own project to another actor. If the latter, for whatever reason, refuses to participate in this allocation of the former's projects responsibilities, or if the owner of the project during the negotiation decides not to allocate the responsibility to this actor, then it is possible that the owner of the project will continue the negotiations with other actors, until he finally allocates this specific responsibility to someone.

Thus, during the negotiations held around a project's specific responsibility, the responsibility itself is transferred from actor to actor, or by using the physics terminology, it draws specific and identifiable orbits from actor to actor, until it is finally allocated to someone. Of course, during the process of negotiation the particular negotiated responsibility can be divided into several parts, into several sub-responsibilities, which are also negotiated and must be allocated to specific actors. Once all project responsibilities have been allocated to specific actors, then the project can be implemented.

The allocation of an actor's project responsibilities refers to the *ex ante* concept of responsibilities, to the *ex ante* determination of what is to be done, and by whom exactly, as far as the actor's project is concerned. And this *ex ante* allocation of responsibilities is a matter of negotiations between actors who use a variety of means in order to allocate or to resist the allocation of specific responsibilities. These means include discursive means, particular practices, and above all, a practical type of knowledge on the issue of the responsibilities allocation, a knowledge that is developed during the negotiation process itself and refers to the actors' familiarity with specific persons, practices, rituals, discourses, etc.' (Papadopoulos, 1995).

Whilst this theoretical and conceptual approach to project analyses (and my own analytical approach is closer to this approach) provides us with a specific and practical approach to the analyses of projects, it still does not, in my view, situate projects within a broader conceptual framework of society and thus, is limited and does not take into account the dynamics of power at play during the different stages of the construction of projects. My argument is that, any analysis that seeks to provide us with some form of clarity on the analyses of projects (for development or any other purpose or goal) would have to take into account the various different social factors that shape the construction of projects. That is, the construction process of projects must be situated within the broader context of development taking into account both internal and external factors that shape development projects. As Edwards (1989: 118-20) commented:

'The natural consequences of a concern for technical interpretations of reality is that knowledge, and the power to control it, become concentrated in the hands of those with the technical skills necessary to understand the language and methods being used... The logical corollary of a world view, which sees development as a series of technical transfers mediated by experts, is that, given a sufficient number of situations or projects in which theses transfers are made, development will occur. But as Sithembiso Nyoni (Zimbabwen Director of Organisation of Rural associations for progress) has pointed out, no country in the world has ever developed itself through projects; development results from a long process of experiment and innovation through which people build up the skills, knowledge and self-confidence necessary to shape their environment in ways that foster progress towards goals such as economic growth, equity in income distribution, and political freedom.

'It is important therefore to explore the effects of particular project interventions not only on target groups and other defined stakeholders but more broadly on hinterland actors, livelihoods and institutions. One must also identify patterns of interaction and accommodation that take place between the different groups of actors, and analyse the ways in which their particular histories, collective memories and time space conceptions shape the reception and outcomes of particular policy measurers. Such studies differ from standard evaluation procedures. Whereas the latter address the fictitious question of whether or not original goals have been reached, the former — based on a broad social impact approach — conceptualises intervention as part (and perhaps only as a minor part) of a wider complex of social practices built upon the interlocking of various actors strategies and intentionalities' (See Long, 2001 and also Olivier de Sardan, 1995: 173-5).

REFERENCES

Bierschenk, Th. (1988) *Development Projects as Arenas of Negotiation for Strategic Groups: A Case from Benin.* Sociologia Ruralis, Vol XXVII: 113-145.

Crehan K. and A. Von Oppen (1988) *Understanding of Development; The Story of Development Projects in Zambia.* Sociologia Ruralis, Vol XXVII: 146-160.

De Haan, H and Long, N (2001) (eds) *Images and Realities of Rural Life.* Van Gorcum & Comp.

Department of Social Development. (2002). *Documenting HIV/AIDS Case Studies in South Africa.* Department of Social Development South Africa, Vol 1.

Dikeni, L. (1996) *Habitat and Struggle: The Case of the Kruger National Park in South Africa.* MSc Thesis Wageningen Agricultural University, Department of Sociology.

Dikeni L., Schoones, I. and Moorehead, R (1996) *Land Use and Environment Policy Dilemmas in the Rangelands of South Africa: Case Studies from the Free State and Northern Province.* L & APC Working Paper 38.

Edwards, M. (1989) *The Irrelevance of Development Studies.* Third world quarterly, 11,1 (January): 116-35.

Long, N (ed.) (1989) *Encounters at the Interface. A perspective on Social Discontinuities in Rural Development.* PUDOC, Agricultural University, Wageningen.

Long, N. (2001) *Development Sociology Actor Perspectives.* London Routledge.

Long, N. and A. Long (Long) (eds.) (1992) *Battle Fields of Knowledge.* Routledge London/New York.

Luckmann and Schutz, T. (1973) *The Structure of The Life World*. Evanston, Illinois: North Western University Press.

Mtubatuba Muncipality (2003) *Integrated Development Plan*. Project Implementation and Performance Management System.

Olivier de Sardan, J.P. (1995) *Anthropologie et Developement: Essai en Socio-anthropologie du Changement Social*. Marseille and Paris: APAD and Karthala.

Papadopoulos, D (1995) *From Negotiations to Networks: A Study of the Responsibilities Orbits at the Interface Between a Rural Bureaucracy and Dynamic Farmers in Greece*. PhD Thesis: Wageningen Agricultural University, Department of Sociology.

Schutz, A. (1962) *The Problem of Social Reality*. The Hague: Nijhoff Publishers.

Van Dusseldorp, D. (1993) *Projects for Rural Development in the Third World: Preparation and Implementation*. Lecture Notes Wageningen Agricultural University, Department of Sociology of Rural Development.

Wallman, S. (1984) *Eight London Households*. London, Routledge.

South African Development Perspectives In Question

CHAPTER 5

The Case of Schmidtsdrift in the Northern Cape of South Africa

Local Knowledge, Development Projects, Planned Intervention, Interpretation, Interests and Livelihoods

INTRODUCTION

As with the previous chapter, this case study attempts to summarise a complex set of findings based on the interpretations, conceptualisations of local actors with regard to the important issues of population, environment and development.

Information contained in various texts on the important issue of population, environment and development is reconciled with a variety of local actors' views and perspectives so as to reach some consensus.

The findings outlined in the previous chapter indicate clearly how complex population, environment and development issues are. The interpretations attached on these issues by the different actors interviewed in this chapter, indicate clearly that different actors located in the various areas of the Northern Cape attach different meanings to these variables on the basis of their set objectives and interests.

Clearly there can be no coherent theoretical definition and/or interpretation of the three variables. Population, environment and development variables have been, and still are, an outcome of social negotiations between various social actors involved in the process of development. They shall remain, and will continue, to interact and conflict with each other in a socially dynamic way.

As often indicated to us by some of the local people interviewed in the field, debating population, development and environment issues in a vacuum is meaningless when there are serious issues of development to deal with. These issues have to be socially contextualised and, more importantly, they have to be informed by social realities on the ground. We believe that this study has attempted to do just what the communities suggested to us.

People in South Africa are increasingly getting anxious about delivery and tangible results and getting tired of endless workshops that lead nowhere. The challenge, therefore, is for the state, development institutions, researchers and other actors working on development projects to provide the opportunity for a focused and productive debate that will seek to reconceptualise the current developmental discourse in South Africa.

As with the other chapters, here the debate on the relations and interactions of the three variables of population, environment and development issues and how these affect different social actors at a local level are being examined with the aim of reconceptualising the current developmental discourse.

The Persistence of Planned Intervention: The Northern Cape Case

The overall objective of the study is to examine the inter-relations between population environment and development, and how these interact and counteract with each other at the local level using two areas (communities) in Kimberley in the Northern Cape — namely Platfontein and Schmidtsdrift.[38]

In each case, population, environmental and development issues are central to the policy debate on the integration of local economies. These plans are clearly spelled out in the Northern

---

38. The farm, Schmidtsdrift is situated about 75 kms outside Kimberley on the Griekwastad road.
39. The IDP document is a report, the main purpose of which is to review whether, and how, the IDP strategic framework and the municipal priorities are being implemented and whether they converge as a general trend.

Cape Sol Plaatje Integrated Development Plan, 2000.[39]

Both area sites currently have a diverse range of land use often adjacent to each other; including large and medium commercial ranches (for both cattle and wildlife), small-scale private farms, the so-called communal areas and large semi-urban settlements (e.g. the townships near Kimberley). In both area sites, significant changes in the broader economy of the Northern Cape are affecting population and environmental trends with major implications for local policy implementation.

A high level of indebtedness typifies most of the white farming sector (as we shall see in one of the remarks made by one farmer later in the study), resulting in shifts in land uses (e.g. from beef to wildlife), consolidation of farm units and diversification of farming operations. In addition to this, the relocation of both ethnic groups from Schmidtsdrift to Platfontein, consequently meant that commercial farmers in the areas under study lost farmworkers.

The development of the mining industry in the form of diamonds and gypsum has also had a great impact on the livelihoods of different local people in the two area sites under study. In other words, these industrial projects have a direct impact on the interaction between the three variables population, environment and development within the Platfontein and Schmidtsdrift areas.

In short, the major impact is on job opportunities for the local people, population pressures on the areas' land surface and on the space these mining projects occupy. These factors have combined to make population, environment and development policy questions particularly complex, with the large, sometimes very large, private holdings providing very few livelihoods under increasingly vulnerable economic conditions for the local people. Of importance here is that, though land as a natural resource has been allocated to the three ethnic groups, it is still leased to commercial white farmers in the areas under study. This is due to a lack of skills in both groups in managing the natural resources.

Understanding the interaction of environment, population and development variables in this case is therefore far from easy. Equally, as we shall see later, the process of implementation of local development policy is one fraught with difficulties. The Northern Cape Provincial and local governments responsible for this have an enormous task ahead.

Current efforts of speeding up the land reform program in South Africa, is not surprisingly, a major priority for government. But how should this go ahead? What are the mechanisms for delivery? What are the implications of this for the environment, population and development discourse within the two research sites under study?

As we shall see later in this chapter, policies are never fixed and/or static if they emerge from discussion, negotiation and sometimes conflict. Linking population, environment and development variables into a coherent policy framework at the different levels of the state remains a challenge for all actors (e.g. non-governmental organisations, the State and business).

In the Northern Cape Case, the key dominant factors that influence the interaction of population, environment and development factors are mainly land-use for ranches (e.g. cattle farming and/or wildlife farming), mining (e.g. diamond and gypsum), infrastructure development and tourism.[40] On all these issues, as the study will show, there are many views and disagreements but little consensus.

This study aims to highlight these views, explore some of the emerging consensus and point to the disagreements, with the aim of setting in train a conceptual and theoretical policy debate on the linkages between environment, population and development variables within the context of the Schmidtsdrift

---

40. A great deal can be said, analysed and written on the history of the !Xu and the Khwe; and especially about how these wider historical processes affect development processes within the research sites under study. However, for the purposes of this study we shall place a focus on the interaction between the three variables of "population", "environment" and "development" and examine how these affect the local people within the areas under study. It is the view of the author that a study of the historical process is a case on its own.

and Platfontein areas. And thus, through this process, question the current development perspectives that shape development practices within the area with the aim of introducing new theoretical concepts for development. The way we went about initiating this debate is outlined in the following sections.

GENERAL FRAME WORK OF THE STUDY

Overall Objectives: According to the State

The relevance of this study is to help provide information to government and the business sector in relation to how government intervention policies are felt and socially interpreted on the ground. Key to this process is the assessment of public sector policies and resultant projects, initiatives and services on the lives of local people and/or local communities, households and individuals.

As in other studies of this nature (see, previous chapter), this study utilises important issues such as employment creation and income generation to assess the impact of state policies on the community (local people) outreach and cost effectiveness of these policies at the local level.

In the field, a wide range of broad and interrelated important research issues and questions emerged (some of which are outlined in the Northern Cape Sol Plaatje Integrated Development Plan 2000, which served as a basis and focus of the study. These are:

+ The profiling of socio-demographic trends (of the areas under study)
+ The identification of government projects and initiatives implemented
+ The establishment of the success of specific initiatives, in terms of declared goals and business plans
+ Determining their impact in relation to reversing

unemployment trends, and also in relation to society and environment

✦ Assessing these impacts in their totality, and also in relation to key contexts such as poverty, education, health, local government and such specific concerns as land use

✦ Assess correctness of targeting, in relation to reported local needs, and in relation to special aspects of delivery

✦ Consider access and communication for such interventions, in an institutional context: What local institutions are able to articulate service demands and short falls to local and national government? Are designated formal institutions responsive? What other institutions exists and are in contact? With which departments are they in contact?

✦ Make the best possible assessment of trend and delivery at a local level: has the delivery of services and benefits under consideration been improving, deteriorating or showing mixed results? How far has the delivery process met its own objectives at a local context and what are the reported reasons?

FRAMEWORK APPROACH

The study seeks to approach these issues and questions from the point of view of different social actors located in different areas of Platfontein and Schmidtsdrift in the Northern Cape Province.

The central argument being that different stakeholders in the areas under study will place different significance on population, environment and development issues and will have different priorities for policy formulation and implementation.

The study identifies social actors according to their relationship to the direct use of the resource, and distinguishes four major groups: the direct users themselves (e.g. large and small-scale commercial farmers and the nature conservation committee); regulators of the use of affected areas (e.g.

provincial government and local municipalities); service providers (e.g. government officials and/or development agencies) and representatives (e.g. elected representatives and members of a community property association).

The findings of the study do not propose new policies that should be implemented in the future: rather they suggest some of the trade offs that have to be addressed in the continuing social negotiations and discussions over existing policy.

THEORETICAL AND CONCEPTUAL FRAMEWORK

This study continues to use the theoretical and methodological framework of previous chapters, viz., the actor-oriented approach. (Long, 2001) develops a synthesis and summary of the concept of the actor-oriented approach. According to him the 'cornerstones of the actor/oriented approach are:

1. Social life is heterogeneous. It comprises a wide diversity of social forms and cultural repertoires, even under seemingly homogeneous circumstances.
2. It is necessary to study how such processes are produced, consolidated and transformed, and to identify the social processes involved, not merely the structural outcomes.
3. Such a perspective requires a theory of agency based upon the capacity of actors to process their and other experiences and to act upon them. Agency implies both certain knowledge-ability, whereby experience and desires are reflexively interpreted and internalised (consciously or otherwise), and the capability to command relevant skills, access to material and non-material resources and engage in particular organising practices.
4. Social action is never an individual ego-centred pursuit. It takes place within the networks of relations (involving

human and non-human components), is shaped by both routine and explorative organising practices and is bounded by certain social conventions, values and power relations.

5. But it would be misleading to assume that such social and institutional constraints can be reduced to general sociological categories and hierarchies based on class, gender, status, ethnicity, etc. Social action and interpretation are context-specific and contextually generated. Boundary markers are specific to particular domains, arenas and fields of social action and should not be prejudged analytically.

6. Meanings, values and interpretations are culturally constructed but they are differentially applied and interpreted in accordance to existing behavioural possibilities or changed circumstances, sometimes generating new cultural 'standards'.

7. Related to these processes is the question of scale, by which I refer to the ways in which micro scale interactional settings and localised arenas are connected to the wider macro scale phenomena and vice versa. Rather than seeing the local as shaped by the global or the global as an aggregation of the local, an actor perspective aims to elucidate the precise sets of interlocking relationships, actor projects and social practices that interpenetrate various social, symbolic and geographical spaces.

8. In order to examine these interrelations it is useful to work with the concept of the social interface which explores how discrepancies of social interest, cultural interpretation, knowledge and power are mediated and perpetuated or transformed at critical points of linkage or confrontation. These interfaces need to be identified ethnographically, not presumed on the basis of pre-determined categories.

9. Thus, the major challenge is to delineate the contours and contents of diverse social forms, explain their genesis and

trace out their implications for strategic social change and modes of consciousness. That is, we need to understand how these forms take shape under specific conditions and in relation to past configurations, with the view to examining their viability, self-generating capacities and wider ramifications.'

As can be seen, therefore, the actor-oriented approach can also be conceptualised as a social interface. It is hence suitable to use the concept of the interface as an appropriate approach for analysing complex problems of environment, population and development in relation to the Platfontein and Schmidtsdrift areas.

Conceptual Frame Work

Evidently the general framework, the framework approach and the theoretical framework of this study are similar, if not identical to the study done on the interrelations between environment, population and development in St Lucia in KwaZulu-Natal, South Africa (see, Chapter 3). This is so because the overall objectives of this study coincide with the general objectives of the study conducted in the Greater St Lucia Wetlands Park. It is also my belief, that, the best theoretical and methodological approaches for dealing with problems of population, development and the environment are the ones adopted in this study.

However, (as we shall see in the sections to follow) the "problematic" and the "problem-holders" of this study differ dramatically from those of the Greater St Lucia Wetlands Park. Of importance to note in this study is that, the "problematic" necessitate the researchers to do brief ethnographic studies within the areas under study. This method also requires open-ended interviews to be done with the various actors involved in the process of development.

This study was based on three weeks of work in the province

of the Northern Cape of South Africa, involving a wide range of discussions and interviews with a variety of social actors dealing with issues of environment, population and development.

As already mentioned, the work was commissioned by the Department of Social Development (DSD) and the problem-holders were the Provincial Ministry of Local Government and the Sol Plaatje Municipality, the Platfontein community and the Schmidtsdrift local communities.

The Provincial Department of Social Development was the host in the initial stages of the study. During the second phase of the study the South African San Institute (SASI) was the host.

In these areas population, environment and development issues are evident and are key dominating factors for the development of the local economy. The following sections of the chapter provide a detailed theoretical and conceptual analysis of our work in the areas under study.

POPULATION, ENVIRONMENT AND DEVELOPMENT: ACTORS' INTERESTS AND PERSPECTIVES

The Local People, the Land and Their Livelihoods

The local people residing in the areas under study are the Bathlaping, the !Xu and the Khwe people, also known as the San people. The Bathlaping people are the land claimants, who were forcefully removed in the early 1980s from their land to make way for the establishment and development of the South African National Defence Force (SANDF) Camp in Schmidtsdrift in the Northen Cape. Most Bathlaping people moved to areas like Douglas, Kuruman and other surrounding areas.

The !Xu and the Khwe were relocated from Namibia and Angola and placed in Schmidtsdrift by the South African Defence Force (SANDF). Most members of the community, especially the men, were members of the South African National Defence Force (SANDF).

The women were mainly there to look after the rest of the family and deal with the different household tasks such as looking after the kids, cleaning the house, etc. The community has lived in the area for years.

In the late 1990s the Bathlaping who were forcefully removed from the area (Schmidtsdrift), reclaimed their land from the new government and were given it back. They now reside in Schmidtdsdrift and have diverse ways of creating livelihoods for themselves.

This process created great pressure on the part of the State to find alternative space for the San. A decision was then taken by the new government to relocate the San people to Plaatfontein, an area close to Kimberley. The San were also given land for farming.

Hence, the main demands of local people in the areas under study, is not for land and/or more land. Their demands are for jobs, the creation of health facilities, the development of infrastructure, the development of better educational facilities, the need for local government structures to provide them with better service and the development of their areas to be sustainable development spaces that can generate wealth in order for them to improve their livelihoods. This was well illustrated to us by one of the community members who resided in Plaatfontein. And he said:

> *... Jy weet (you know) ... The government has done a good job in relocating us to Plaatfontein and providing us with housing. Previously we used to live in tents, like canned Sardines... there was no proper sanitation for us in Schmidtsdrift, no water and no educational facilities for our children... At least now we have some houses... There are some plans to develop a school and some clinics on the pipe-line... Mandela het tog maar vir ons gehelp (Mandela has really helped us.) (My own translation.)* **(Fieldwork notes, 2004)**

Another resident residing in Schmidtsdrift puts it this way.
He said:

'...Bona (you see) ... Leslie... We are very happy to have received
our land, after so many years of waiting. We have been living
in other people's places for too long, living without jobs for too
long; we have lost our cattle in places like Kuruman and
Douglas because of forced removals by the previous
government... Now we are back on our land again... Here we
can farm with our cattle again, we can do mining and we can
plant vegetables like we did before... What we now need is
houses and schools for our children...* (**Fieldwork notes, 2004**)

These views gain support from one of the South African San
Institute's (SASI) officials. And he said:

... It is quite true the state has provided the different
communities with land and space for them to make a living
from. My problem is that this has happened more than ten
years ago and there is still no development taking place... Take
the problem of infrastructural development, a basic necessity
and a human rights issue..

The people in Plaatfontein do not even have toilets, the
rubbish is piling up there and no one seems to care. Our local
government people do not even seem to know that there are
problems like that facing the community... There does not seem
to be any plans set in place for providing people with such
services. We recently had to transform one of the buildings in
the area for people to use as a clinic... and mobilise some of the
healthworkers to work there... and provide people with health
services... (**Fieldwork notes 2007**)

Most people interviewed about their livelihood strategies
mentioned the Community Property Association (CPA) as one
that helps them financially. Others survive through various state

support grants like the pension fund schemes provided by the state for the elderly. Most others had to look for jobs outside the areas under study. Unemployment is rife within all the areas under study. See the section below for a further detailed analysis of the economic and livelihood strategies employed by the different members of the communities.

Commercial Beef Farmers and the Land

Cattle ranchers aim to make a profit from their enterprise. This may be done in a number of ways. Cattle ranchers include those who keep animals for meat (e.g. sale of weaners) and those who run stud farms and sell breeding animals. This section will focus on red meat production, as this dominates the sector within the two research sites.

Maximising profits from the sale of red meat means ensuring high levels of weight gain. Weight gain may be maximised per animal or per unit area. Most beef ranchers spoken to aim for stock rates, which maximise total meat production from their farms where animals must be in prime condition to ensure highest possible calving rate.

Beef ranchers argue that this stocking strategy coincides with range conservation and sustainable production, as sensible economics and sound environmental management coincide in beef enterprise. Thus, low stock rates mean high-quality pasture and so high returns from beef animals. Ranchers argued if this is managed sensitively, ensuring that stock numbers are regulated in accordance with shifts in grass species composition, degradation is avoided and a highly sustainable system is created.

Some of the ranchers interviewed argued that some form of rotational or resting grazing system was essential. This allowed ease of management, as well as the possibility of allowing grass to recover if overused. Most ranchers visited had invested in camp or paddock fencing. Most fencing had been installed during the past thirteen years at a considerable expense and, in most cases, continued to be maintained by the state. As one rancher, member and manager of the CPA explained:

> ... *These people (!Xu and Khwe) do not have much farming experience; they have not worked on the land for many years like me... They are trekkers, that is where their expertise lies. You cannot just put cattle here and think you are finished with your job. There are many things to consider and take into account. For example, you may have land for cattle grazing here, but you cannot keep the cattle there forever, you must keep on changing according to the change of the season, because in winter there is not enough grass to feed the cattle. But there might be enough vegetation to feed wildlife. Sometimes you may just want the land to recover and grow grass... These are some the things I always have to explain to them...* (**Fieldwork Notes, 2007**)

As with all other producers in dry-land areas, variable rainfall and drought are key constraints to the production system. Most people commented that low rainfall often hit them severely. While ranchers articulated a desire to stock at low rates in low rainfall areas in accordance with a conservative stocking strategy, they realise that this is not enough to ensure that their expected income is maintained. This type of strategy, supported by research and government programmes in the past, is increasingly realised to be unviable.

Many beef farmers have taken on very large debts, some have changed their operations completely (e.g. shifting to game ranching), others are diversifying into other income earning activities, and some have sold up and left the sector completely.

These family businesses contrast with a few very large operations, which are buffered to some degree by the sheer scale of the business, the ability to raise credit on good terms, and the fact that the farming enterprise is part of a large holding company.

The commercial farmers suggested a number of options in the discussions on strategies to deal with drought and rainfall variability. According to them, three contradictory options were open to them; either you could over-stock and hope that the land will cope, or you could rely on external support through government subsidy or loans from commercial banks, or you could diversify into other income earning activities, adding value to existing operations (e.g. selling biltong, providing tourists with opportunities for hunting etc.), or joining a game ranching consortium. In the area under study where most commercial farmers are located, most farmers opted for the last option.

In this case, these farmers (mainly three farmers), lease land from the CPA for the purposes of game farming. In this way they can make profit through game farming. According to them, this is better than relying on external funding in the form of commercial loans from commercial lenders and from the state. As one farmer, from the Community Property Association (CPA) explains this organisational system:

'.. You see I am the farm manager for the CPA, which means I work for them. However, I am also a Commercial farmer and farm cattle. The land does not belong to me, it belongs to the Community Property Association, they own the land and I work for them. This is good for me, because I do not have to rely on the state and the financial institutions... Besides Beef farmers in the area are indebted... Beef Farming is an expensive venture...* (**Fieldwork Notes, 2007**)

Service Provision

Extensive research on technical issues relating to beef production has been carried out in the country since the 1930s. This has covered a whole range of issues from grazing systems to animal production, and in a wide diversity of agro ecological conditions. This research has formed the basis of recommendations and the ideas have largely been incorporated into practice. Thus virtually all ranchers used to stock at recommended rates, many followed rotational grazing systems, and most have introduced standard animal production practices. Research and extension provision to this sector was therefore exemplary. It was demand led, tackling problems of concern to producers, and was effective; ensuring that ideas from research are available and inclusive. It employed people from the sector in both extension and research and gave deep insights into its operations. Moreover, in the past the policy framework was highly supportive of this sector, providing extensive subsidies for capital development, as well as support during drought periods.

However, the opposite is happening at present. As one informant who is a commercial farmer and is a member of the CPA explained:

> ... Before [1994], our government used to look after our land, they used to monitor everything you do, interfere in anything you do, assist and give you advice on how much you must stock, when to stock and help with drought problems when necessary... However, now it is free for all, you can do what you like and when you like with no interference and there is also no guidance from government on anything... (**Fieldwork notes 2007**)

Small Scale Farmers and the Land

Closely linked but distinct to the commercial farmers described above and to communal farmers are the small-scale farmers. Small-scale farmers are distinguished from producers on communal areas by the fact that, they own a discreet area of land either singly or in small groups. They endeavour to make fulltime livelihood from farming, although this is not always possible and they often have off farm activities. These farmers both raise livestock and often venture into other small economic activities.

These circumstances oblige small-scale farmers to practice dual stock-raising practices. On the one hand, to maximise their cash income from livestock, they raise animals for red meat production. On the other, as insurance against risks and as a form of savings, they maintain as many animals as possible on the range.

In terms of grazing strategies these farmers thus both pursue opportunistic strategies to benefit from range production in good years (and be left with at least some animals in bad years), and to some extent practice conservative stocking rates to enhance beef production. For the former they monitor total production of their animals and for the latter they manage the range in order to promote weight gain in their animals.

Small-scale producers therefore tend to have a higher amount of animals on the range than the present carrying capacity norms advise, but the stocking rate is lower, at the extreme, than a level at which animals begin to die. In the Northern Cape, especially in the two research sites, it was very difficult to ascertain what the actual different impact small-scale farming activities have on the range from that of commercial farmers.

Service Provision

According to most farmers spoken to, the key main service provider supporting small-scale farmers in the area is the provincial Department of Agriculture. The key areas of service that the department provides to farmers are in terms of technology and research.

However, a common concern amongst most small-scale farmers in the area was that the services of the Department of

Agriculture were provided in a top-down fashion, which did not fully take into account the realities on the ground. Thus, the services were mainly based on agricultural support systems that favoured cattle grazing only and did not support other farming activities such as game ranching and/or wildlife farming. To them, cattle grazing was supporting the needs of large commercial farmers. According to one farmer:

> ... OK! Government people are very good in helping us in terms of agricultural advice, agricultural tools and telling us what we need to do in order for us to maintain livestock. However, they do not understand that some of us, if not most of us, are already trying to make a living through game. For them there is only one thing for this area; cattle farming... cattle farming... Leslie; a friend of mine often receives tourists from overseas who only want to come here and see the game and others who like the adventure of hunting and having fun with their families. They see us for that and not for our cattle; cattle farming for them is one boring activity. He was telling me that, with a few tourists who are interested in game watching and hunting you can make more money than farming with cattle... You can feed your workers by giving them the meat; you can earn money through transporting the visitors and providing them with accommodation. All this can be done at low cost... However, despite all of this, the government only sees one form economic venture for all of us, and that is, cattle farming. They do not take into account what we see on the ground, they are stuck in their own ideas... They must learn to experiment all the time and listen to us... (**Fieldwork Notes, 2004**)

Game Ranchers and the Environment

The major objectives of Game ranchers are to achieve maximum profit from managing the range through raising wildlife, primarily large ungulates. They achieve this through a variety of activities like ecotourism, the sale of live animals, the production of biltong, the manufacture of handicrafts and curios, the production of thatching grass and the provision of accommodation for visitors.

Game ranchers raise a diverse mix of animals, bulk grazers, selective grazers, non-selective grazers and browsers of both indigenous and exotic species in order to maintain the highest stocking level on their farms, commensurate with maintaining a sustainable supply of grass and forage. They argue that this wide range of species enables them to make a highly efficient use of natural vegetation so as to achieve profitability, maintain sustainability and contribute towards the conservation of bio-diversity.

The grazing strategies that the game ranchers pursue are effectively somewhere between conservative stocking rates and opportunistic strategies. Their concern is principally with running the highest number of a diverse mix of wildlife on their ranches. As such, they are concerned with the monitoring of the total production of animals. But to an extent, they are also interested in live animal sales and they also monitor range condition and raise animals for weight gain.

This might be especially true with exotic species being raised in habitats foreign to them: the need to maintain them through difficult periods (i.e. during cold months at high altitudes) implies a need for rich pasture to keep them in optimum condition. Perimeter fencing is essential for the ranch and, rather than using internal fencing, game ranchers have socially developed, sophisticated systems of mobile exclusion to manipulate the access of wildlife to fodder and grazing.

This demonstrates that game ranchers manipulate a mix of range management strategies. In order to maintain sufficient numbers of a wide range of species as an attraction for eco-tourism, their strategy is to maintain as high a stocking rate as possible implying many animals, but little grass. Whereas for biltong production, live sales and to maintain adult male trophy-bearing animals, they are concerned with weight gain and the best condition of the individual animals, implying fewer animals and the maintenance of quality grass species and sophisticated rotational grazing systems.

The diversified output from game ranches (ecotourism, live sales, etc.) often involves value being added on the farm by more labour-intensive means than in the commercial livestock sector, and hence leads to more employment opportunities than in the commercial sector or in the protected area management.

This is seen not only in the ecotourism activities and in the accommodation for visitors to game ranches, but is also true for the complex management system (involving mobile fencing, live animal capture, etc.) needed to manage this kind of range. As one farmer explains this labour intensive process:

> ... I would give game ranching fifty percent of a chance to prosper in this area and, also give cattle farming the same percentage. However, I guarantee you, that game ranching can employ more people than cattle farming. For example, if all these areas could be used for game farming, I could create jobs for game guards, trackers, game guides, camp cleaners, cooks, set up an administrative office, have my chalets and employ people to keep them clean... In this way I can employ a whole lot of these people [!Xu and Khwe]... (**Fieldwork notes, 2007**)

Game ranchers argue that their production system is environmentally efficient, sustainable (through complex management practices and through the use of a range of adopted species) and highly productive (the range of adapted species allows a high stocking rate).

Service Provision

Given the fact that game farming has only been a recent discovery in the area and only a few farmers in the areas under study are practising game farming, the State in the form of local government has not invested much research in this area of farming. Neither is there any form of organised assistance for game farmers in terms of technology transfer or otherwise. The only form of notable service comes from the nature conservation department.

The department hopes to transfer some wildlife from other conservation camps in the country to the areas under study. This is so because the National Department of Environment and Tourism (DEAT) has identified some areas where, due to overgrazing and other problems, the carrying capacity of those conservation areas cannot cope with the species located there.

Hence, instead of culling and/or using other methods of extinction, the best option is to transfer the species. The communities in the Northern Cape have been earmarked as local people who can benefit from such schemes.

Communal Farmers and the Environment

Our open-ended interviews (and ethnographic observations) with the Bathlaping communities in a community meeting that took place in 2004 in Schmidtsdrift confirmed that communal farmers represent a whole range of different people, with a variety of interests and a diversity of livelihoods.[41] For the most part, they lived in the surrounding areas making part of their living from farming on small pieces of land.

Livestock production is therefore only part of their livelihood strategy and is important for only a subset of the total population. Other activities include some arable and gardening activities, local off-farm piecework, small-scale businesses (spaza shops) and trading operations, as well as remittances, pensions and other sources of income from elsewhere.

---

41. This meeting was organised by the Community Property Association (CPA) and the CSIR. The broad objectives of the meeting were to look at the after-effects of relocation in the country; Schmidtsdrift was one such area. The Bathlaping community were returning back to their land and the !Xu and the Khwe were being relocated during that time.

One resident, formerly from Kuruman and presently residing in Schmidtsdrift explained:

... We were removed here by the South African Defence Force many years ago. Previously, we used to farm here and live in great harmony amongst ourselves. Many of us moved to places like Kuruman, Douglas and some people to as far as Kimberley. Now we are back, after winning our claim and still they have not finally given these other people their land back... Some are not here, they are still coming; we need to still find them...
(**Fieldwork Notes 2004**)

Residents interviewed in areas like Kuruman and Douglas live, for the most part, on marginal incomes. Many suffer extreme degrees of poverty, certainly by comparison to other land users in the areas under study. Their objectives, therefore, must be focused on securing a livelihood in the face of great insecurity. To do this, most make use of a diverse range of activities including part-time farming. Livestock in these settings is seen for its multiple values. For example, cattle are important for their milk and sometimes for their draught power, manure and meat. They are also important as security and may be significant for ritual purposes.

By contrast, the commercial beef producers keep animals for quite different, and much more diverse, reasons. Numbers, rather than meat production per unit area or animal, are important and so people argue that they want as many animals as possible.

This is, of course, constrained by available grazing land as well as herding labour, but the principle of maintaining high stocking rates is central to their broader livelihood security objectives. As one resident from Kuruman, now residing in Schmidtsdrift related his observations to us:

... Our situation is different here, we farm with cattle; these animals feed on grass and water. If water is there animals can graze and when grass is found there... they move on ... The

total number of animals in the area is not regulated and controlled, although the problem for us is… animals often go to different places or split… Different types of animals splitting all the time can create problems for you when herding… Which means; you need more man for herding them and making sure they are not going to be stolen by some people residing outside the area…' (**Fieldwork Notes, 2004**)

Variable rainfall and drought are thus the main constraints to the production of livestock on the communal range. Strategies of dealing with this are further limited for those living in areas like Kuruman and Douglas by severe shortages of available grazing land, small herd sizes and insecure income streams. These conditions, combined with their different livelihood objectives, make communal area livestock producers manage their herds in quite a different way to commercial beef ranchers. Instead of holding stock numbers at a low and relatively constant level, communal areas herds fluctuate widely with available forage. In short, when rainfalls are high and there is no drought, communal farmers believe that they can prosper and when drought occurs and there is a shortage of rain they believe that they cannot prosper.

Since communal area producers must operate under such constrained conditions, with limited access to land and capital in particular, management systems turned to be low cost and fairly labour intensive.

Social and economic ties within communities afford opportunities for labour-sharing arrangements, particularly for herding. The grazing system in Schmidtsdrift is communally held by the Bathlaping community, with identifiable boundaries, rules and regulations governing exclusions. Grazing management, like in most communal grazing areas, is flexible with a mixture of free range grazing and herding depending on the location and the season.

In the absence of fencing, social rules identify grazing area boundaries, but these are often not rigid and are usually open to some form of negotiation. A flexible form of communal tenure thus allows a low cost route to managing livestock without the need to invest in expensive locking systems. But as labour availability decreases, especially through increased access to schooling for children and greater demands for adults, fencing is regarded as an increasingly important component of the communal management system.

Another notable and apparent feature of this fencing system emerged during our process of conducting interviews in the area amongst the Bathlaping. In almost every interview we had with the members of the community the need for fencing was mentioned. This was because of the conflicts between the Bathlaping community who were being resettled in the Schmidtsdrift area and some members of the !Xu and Khwe who were still waiting to be resettled at Platfontein. The Bathlaping at the time accused the other groups of cattle theft and immediately resolved that to solve the problem, fencing would the best solution. As one community member explained the problem to us:

> ... The problem is that we all know that fencing is expensive and we cannot really afford it. However, with the rate of thefts that are taking place in the area it is better for government to build us fences, in that way, we cannot accuse each other... If we continue in this way there will be nothing left of us. **(Fieldwork notes, 2004)**

Service Provision

Most service provision to the Bathlaping community is contradictory and sometimes confusing. Sometimes it comes from the State and at times from some commercial farmer and/or NGO in the form of advice.

However, what can be noted is that when the service comes

from the State and/or a commercial farmer it comes with some set of assumptions. These include: the communal area is being degraded by excessive livestock populations, the area is not suitable for grazing with livestock, the actual owners of livestock must always be present to take care of their stock (in short, they must not venture into other business opportunities outside the area) and not ask their extended family to take care of the stock when he/she is away; livestock production is backward and needs to be modernised.

These assumptions, in turn, inform the type of extension service that is provided, as well as the thinking about policy. As one commercial beef rancher puts it:

... This people do not know anything about farming... How can the state place them here with no farming skills? Some of them do not live here, but they have cattle here. They live in Johannesburg and ask someone else to look after their stock... You cannot run farming in that way... This is what I told one MEC... (**Fieldwork notes, 2007**)

A very confusing and centrally directed approach to development and technology transfer emerges from the provincial and local government level. As one official explained to us:

... We have plans for the Bathlaping, we know what they need and we know their problems... They need to develop eco-tourism, game farming; and we must make sure that they get the necessary technology for that... They must be provided with help so that they can help in the development of the local economy... However, they have no understanding of eco-tourism and how this can benefit them. So we have allowed them to carry on with cattle farming, maybe it's the best for them... However, we must deliver in that area... That is our mandate as government... (**Fieldwork notes, 2004**)

Provincial Nature Conservation Board (Protected Area Managers) and the Range Land

As already discussed in the previous section, the primary objectives of the managers of protected areas are to conserve biodiversity, act as stewards of a national and international heritage, maintain protected areas as reservoirs of wildlife and protect the option values of wildlife and biodiversity for future generations. They also endeavour to increase the awareness of the public on conservation through tourism, educational programmes and through the media. The Northern Cape Nature Conservation Service is responsible for this function.

At its most extreme, protected area management of "total exclusion zones" implies no management at all of the range, leaving wildlife populations to thrive and perish in line with fodder, pasture and water availability. In practice, this form of management is becoming increasingly rare and protected area managers are becoming more and more active in the control of wildlife populations and feed availability

To maintain diverse populations of wildlife and maintain biodiversity, particularly in dry areas such as the Northern Cape, protected area managers need vast areas of space to exploit. These areas needs to be free of fences within a perimeter so as to allow wildlife using different parts of the range to move to where their feed is found in different seasons of the year. Part of the objectives of protected area managers is to prevent poaching within the range and to make sure that the range is used only for the wildlife.

Service Provision

As can be observed in the study of St Lucia, protected area managers are service providers themselves and have developed sophisticated technologies for wildlife management (culling, monitoring, animal capture, etc.) and for the effective control of park boundaries. They are increasingly providing tourism facilities and extension services in environmental services aimed at the young.

In the areas under study, the Nature Conservation Service has been working with the Bathlaping community in Smichdtsdrift. As one member of the conservation service committee explained to us:

... We recognise the potential of this area for game ranching venture in preference to livestock farming. After much consultation with the planning consultants, the returning communities and politicians; the Trust has indicated that it wishes to develop 10 000 hectares of the area for game ranching and/or ecotourism as a means of sustainable development...

The project enjoys the support of government and the wider community of the Kimberley district... You see... The Provincial Cabinet of the Northern Cape has allocated R770 000 from the Provincial Discretionary Fund of the Reconstruction and Development Programme (RDP) for the development of the project...

... Verstaan jy. The Schmidtsdrif Trust is already a member of the Kimberley Triangle forum which is a wider initiative of local landowners West of Kimberley who are developing a plan to cooperatively develop and manage an area 124 000 hectares, including a national park, as a consolidated wildlife utilisation area... This will constitute the second largest area in South Africa. Where the big five Elephant, Rhino, Leopard, Lion and Buffalo could become part of Northern Cape species... Plus our area has an advantage of being Malaria free... (My own Translation) **(Fieldwork notes 2004)**

The Mining Industry Environment and the People

Miners, like business people, aim to make profits from their mining activities. In the case of the Northern Cape there are two forms of minerals that can be exploited for this purpose. These are diamonds and gypsum. Key to the objectives of mining industries is to supply raw materials for processing to both international and local dealers.

Mining industries in the areas under study do not own any land, however they lease land from the Community Property Association (in other words, from the local people).

According to most people spoken to in the areas, the mining industry benefits them in terms of jobs. However, the problem is that there is very little transparency on how much profit the mining industry makes through its various activities. Even the Community Property Association (CPA) is not aware of what profits the mining industry is making within the area.

Although it's difficult to measure the impact of the mining industry in terms of environmental degradation in the area and how this affects the ecosystem in the areas under study, a common concern for health problems caused by the industry can be found from all actors involved in the development process of the area.

This problem, according to the different actors, requires monitoring by the State. The State is in a better condition to monitor this problem. Equally, the State has a responsibility to ensure that revenue derived from the mining activities benefits the local people. According to them, leasing of land does not guarantee an equitable share of revenue for the community.

Finally, most of the Bathlaping people were concerned about mining being seen as the only source of revenue creation. In their view, 'mining is not a long-term sustainable economic venture. Mines are only good as long as they can produce mineral resources; when the mineral resources are depleted then they are useless ...' Hence, the need for them to maximise their own profit through other economic ventures like cattle farming.

According to one informant, who previously worked in the mines as a labourer for a few years:

> ... *To tell you the truth, I used to work in the mines a few years ago... Mining is like the water provision system provided to us in the township by government. Say for example, you fetch water early in the morning from a tap [which is a few kilometres from your house] and you bring them home. The water must serve about five people in the house; you all drink, wash and cook with the water for the evening and finish. The following morning there is no water in the house and then you are stranded... Also sometimes the taps in the townships runs dry and there is no water... Or maybe if you are a woman and you are breast feeding your baby and your breasts runs out of milk and then you are forced to use powder milk which can also sometimes have health consequences for your child. When the powder milk is finished then, what do you do...? That is how I see mining compared to cattle farming. Besides we do not even own these mines...* (**Fieldwork Notes 2004**)

Residents sited the importance of the Vaal River as a source of sustainability. This is so, because according to them, the Vaal River is used for fishing, to irrigate the crops that are near the river and to provide water for their livestock through windmills. Hence, the concern for the impact the mining industries may have on the river.

Discussion / Analysis

In this study, an attempt is being made to summarise a complex set of findings based on the interpretations and conceptualisations of a variety of local actors with regard to the important issue of population, environment and development in the Northern Cape of South Africa.

Information contained in different texts on the important issue of population, environment and development is reconciled with a variety of local actors' views and perspectives, so as to reach some consensus on the issue.

The findings outlined in the previous section of this study, indicate clearly how complex population, environment and development issues are within the context of the Northern Cape.

The interpretations attached to these issues by the various actors interviewed indicate clearly that different actors located in the various areas of the Northern Cape (Plaatfontein, Schmidtsdrift) attach different meanings to the three variables. Of relevance, is that each actor/set of actors gives meaning to the variables on the basis of their set objectives and interests.

Clearly there can be no coherent theoretical definition and/or interpretation of the three variables. The population, environment and development variables have been and still are an outcome of social negotiations between various actors involved in the process of development. They shall remain, and will continue to interact and conflict with each other in a socially dynamic way.

The findings and interpretations contained in the previous sections of this study suggest a possible way that the policy process on population, environment and development could move forward at the local (municipality) level in the Northern Cape.

This study in a very preliminary way, tried to create a focus for discussion around key policy issues dealing with issues of population, environment and development within Plaatfontein and Schmidtsdrift in the Northern Cape Province.

As often indicated to us in this study by some of the local people interviewed in the field, there is no need for debating population, environment and development issues in a vacuum when they have serious issues of development to deal with. These issues have to be contextualised, actor bounded, and more importantly they have to be informed by social realities on the ground. We believe that this study has in many ways attempted to do just what the communities suggested to us.

In using the concept of the actor-oriented approach, I found that despite clear challenges for the state in terms of its intervention and governance practices at a regional level, there is a need for the state to provide the opportunity for a focused and productive debate on the relations and interactions of the three variables of population environment and development issues within a framework of a policy platform where specific policy action can be taken.

There is also a need for a theoretical re-conceptualisation of the development discourse with the region. In the next section of this chapter we will explore these issues further.

State Intervention Practices

Within the areas under study, there appears to be areas where clear action by government is possible. Around some of these issues a fairly clear consensus seems to be emerging. The government could move ahead quite quickly on these issues, at least by testing out options, if not tackling more fundamental areas of policy, such as revising the remit of certain government tasks or, more basically, through legislative reform. While other issues still have obstacles requiring further debate and discussion, the issues on which clear consensus have emerged are:

1. Risk is an inevitable part of dry land farming activities, but risk management strategies require some degree of support from government if livelihoods are to be sustained in the face of drought. This does not necessarily mean high levels of drought subsidy to certain sections of the population, but external support may be more effectively directed at encouraging diversification. This may mean employment

generating, on-farm activities (e.g. adding value to existing farm products) or diversification to off-farm activities. This applies to the entire spectrum of rural producers, but the greatest attention needs to be paid to the more vulnerable groups.

2. The use of universal planning norms, such as carrying capacity, does not make sense. There is a need to move towards more local planning, involving much more discussion with local land users and a more participative planning that recognises the livelihood requirements of the various people. This requires a major overhaul of the agricultural and farm planning approach, the need to provide assistance to both wildlife and commercial beef farmers, and the training of agricultural extension officers to provide assistance to all the different farming groups.

3. Unlike in most other provinces in South Africa, where the major demands on the land reform programme are based on property rights, in the Northern Cape (within the areas under study) this is no longer the case. Rather, the demands are centred around livelihood issues, service delivery and the need for better management of their natural resources.

4. There are a diversity of land tenure types, which are continuously evolving. The policy focus should be less on property rights *per se*, but more on resource access management. This suggests that land reform approaches need to consider a wide range of property types and expand beyond the current focus on the relocation of property to private smaller units.

5. The three communities, in their different capacities, in the Northern Cape should have the opportunity to benefit from such resources, through some product harvesting, employment opportunities and revenue sharing. Government, therefore, needs to invest in capacity building for the communities residing in the areas under study in the Northern Cape, in skills of wildlife management, tourist

development, etc.

6.   The point about the diversification of farming practices cannot be emphasised enough here. As the findings indicate, clearly there is a need to think beyond the use of the range land in terms of cattle farming and/or wildlife farming. All three communities are already thinking of using diverse forms of range land usage.

Planned Intervention Practices

While there is great concern amongst all actors interviewed about service provision by the State within the areas under study, it is not clear to them who exactly is responsible for the poor services provided to them. This disagreement is particularly evident amongst the Plaatfontein and Schmidtsdrift residents.

The state, however, has established a development committee comprising of different government departments responsible for environment, population and development issues to coordinate its activities regarding the development process in the two areas under study. On another level, the State also has the Sol Plaatje Municipality, whose major task is to service these areas.

The key issue here is, who is really responsible for providing service to the three areas? Is it the development committee or, is it the municipality? There seems to be general disagreement amongst all three communities — and amongst government officials — over this issue.

The challenge, therefore, is to reach agreement amongst State actors, to clarify the different roles that the different State organs need to play with regards to service provision to the three actors. This needs to be communicated clearly to the three communities by the State.

Brief Analysis

The debate on population, environment and development must be informed by local dynamics and challenges for development, as opposed to being an abstract debate that is not informed by praxis.

Equally, the process of policy change and the implementation thereof is one that must be reconceptualised from the current conceptualisation of policy intervention practice existing within the area under study. The current approach visualises policy intervention rather as being top-down and linear.

This study has highlighted how population, environment and development variables socially interact, counteract and at times conflict with each other in many ways in Schmidtsdrift and Plaatfontein in the Northen Cape of South Africa. Clearly, the policy challenges are different for each area under study.

Different histories, different ecologies, different economic conditions and different people mean that different policies will be appropriate for different places. However, it is evident in the findings that there are a number of themes that appear to be common on both sites. The cross-cutting themes of carrying capacity and land degradation, risk management and livelihoods, economic and livelihood units, tenure and property rights, conservation options and community approaches highlighted in this chapter appear to be central to the debate on the inter-linkages between environment, population and development in both areas.

REFERENCES

Dikeni, L. (2003), *Population, Environment and Development: Actors Perspective — The Case of St Lucia.* Unpublished Study.

Long, N (ed.) (1989) *Encounters at the Interface. A Perspective on Social Discontinuity in Rural Development.* PUDOC, Agricultural University, Wageningen.

Long, N. and A. Long (Long) (eds.) (1992) *Battle Fields of Knowledge.* Routledge. London/New York.

Long, N. (2001) *Development Sociology Actors Perspective*s. Routledge.

Sol Plaatje Municipality (2000) *Integrated Development Plan, Project Implementation and Performance Management System.*

INDEX